"Now, Interpret This!"

Dream Journal

"Now, Interpret This!"

Dream Journal

www.nowinterpretthis.com

A daily dream journal to document
your night dreams.

Thanks to my beloved NIT Staff for your
supreme effort and research for the included
"Now, Interpret This!"
Symbol Library
And thank you for **all** you do!
You rock!

Melody Paasch

Table of Contents

Introduction

How dreams can help determine your destiny

Ever wonder what transpires in other realms while you dream? You're about to find out—and your new insights will be powerful enough to transform you and change your life forever in ways large and small, all of them good.

Interactions, transactions and commissions take place during the dreaming process. Too many dreamers miss these critical engagements simply because they don't recognize the impact of what's playing out during sleep.

Here is some information that will help. I'll open a portal of greater understanding and give ample reason to *listen to your dreams.*

Instruction helps at every level

Anyone who has developed effective skills has done so by honing natural talents. For some, the gift was imparted by others who are established in the same realm. Your "calling" (or propensity) to a destiny and talent comes from your intrinsic nature; it's there **by design, stamped into your DNA**. And it's your passion for your calling (intrinsic gifts and talents) that cultivates and sharpens you so you can touch and transform those with whom you come into contact (one-to-one, in groups, even virtually in cyberspace).

The sad thing is that natural gifts can lie dormant for years, decades, even lifetimes. Those who have talents, pro-actively engage them, and discern how to use them wisely **gain more robust talent as time goes on**.

Overlooking, or trying to stifle, the talent/passion/gifting you were born with will always (always!) leave a nagging sense of discontent. **You'll always be longing to fulfill your central destiny, your onboard North Star**.

How diligently you focus on and "exercise" your gift will dictate its effectiveness. To win in sports, play an instrument or learn a new language, you have to practice to get better. And although being deemed (or considering yourself) a "natural" sounds easy-as-pie, you have to look deeper to realize how much practice and passion it takes for "naturals" to become outstanding star performers and transformers. Nothing worth doing or being comes easily (or everybody could do it!), but it can certainly come a lot easier than it usually does. Your dreams are doing everything in their power to help you along, but unless you're listening to them and accurately discerning what they're telling you, they can remain as mysterious as ancient hieroglyphics!

Instruction gives you a starting point on the way to understanding
The instruction students receive offers a frame of reference upon which to build a solid structure. *It's simply a starting place.* Your reservoir fills as you study. The originator of the messages you receive offer you an opportunity to discover, try out and practice your intrinsic resources. You grow and succeed based on how much you learn and what you ultimately decide to do with the information.

The only entity capable of helping you fully understand your dreams is your onboard dream maker. This is why it's essential to engage with the source that creates your dream messages. *The source knows the heart, motive and origin of* **all** *spirit-based communication.* The source is your Creator, the One who creates, initiates and engages everything that has life.

The messages in your dreams are often "Creator" messages
Your Creator will author some of your dream messages and will use others for His purposes. It can be crucial to your success in strategic areas to fully understand the messages your dreams are telling you. What do they mean? Why do you have them?

Not every dream is from the heart of your Creator, obviously. But Creator can (and does) use everything that is sent by others to disorient or disturb you. He is bigger than every opposing force in your life and in the spirit realm. He delights in using attacks against you to strengthen and catapult you to further advancement. The result: your enemy will eventually regret ever messing with you in the first place. He'll have to "eat" what he dishes out at some point. Good news, huh? I think so...

Dreams and You

Are you a prolific dreamer?
If you dream often and have lucid (cognitive, vivid) dreams you may have the "gift of dreams". This is vastly different from "just dreaming". Everyone dreams whether or not they remember or dwell on them. Those with the "gift of dreams" may also be "seers", too: one who "sees" into the spirit realm via visions or by seeing through a veil that opens to them. Sound familiar? You may have the gift, if so!

The Nature of Dreams
Some dreams have multiple messages and at times they offer messages linked to a particular time or season in a dreamer's life. Your dreams will often unfold through familiar colloquialisms. They may convey messages in your own dialect. This is because the story belongs to you, the dreamer, so your dreams will rarely deliver messages in a foreign vernacular. Expect to connect in some way with the vocabulary of your dreams…sometimes even in an obviously amusing way and the central, guiding message is usually simpler than you expect.

Look for "play" on words, idioms and translations of statements that have meant something within your life experiences. Watch for puzzle pieces that connect one story line to another from the same night's dreams. There will be times when every dream during a single night or time period will be connected; other times the only connection will be within the variable scenes within a single dream.

The data that fills your reservoir lends itself to a language that you can understand. For example, if I watch "The Matrix" before going to bed, I may well dream of being unplugged from a false reality. It doesn't mean that the movie necessarily colors or influences the message. The movie merely offers data that frames an opportunity for me to process information based on a familiar or current experience. The experience includes information, which connects with one or more sites of personal perception, setting the stage for a similar story line.

Creator will speak your language, but you may not understand the central message without taking some initiative to engage with your dream, to unwrap it.

Just as it's prudent to learn another language before you travel to a foreign country for an extended period, it's prudent to learn your dream language so you can operate fluently within its culture. To navigate your dreams without hitting a shoal, you may need to learn to translate the messages you receive. Remember, this isn't nuclear science. The adventure of unwrapping your dream must be Spirit-led.

Déjà vu's

Déjà vu (vividly feeling you've experienced the same scene and experience before) is simply a 411 (information call) letting you know you're in the right place at the right time. The "key" to any déjà vu experience you have is to get the information you need to fulfill your greatest existence in that moment. It may strictly be a confirmation that the time is right for something transformational to occur, but it can also be an invitation to respond to achieve a particular outcome. What should you do at moments like these? How should you respond to déjà vu moments?

During déjà vu moments, there is usually an opportunity to fulfill a particular assignment—and there is often a reward. Sometimes it's as simple as releasing an encouraging word to someone in the room that brightens their day. These aren't moments you want to overlook—ever. It's important to realize the power of communication in your dreams and the gifts you're offered. Can you recall a déjà vu moment when you wondered what it "meant", why you were experiencing this heightened sense of the here and now? Were you mystified by the experience, wondering what to do with it? During déjà vu moments, be willing to receive fresh sensitivity to Creator's nudge!

Try to recall and cite déjà vu moments where you've experienced an acute awareness of the time you were standing in; how it may have connected to a dream or vision you may have received. Could you have responded with an appropriate action in that moment? Did you?

Notes:

_____

_____

_____

_____

_____

_____

_____

_____

Messages in Dreams/Dream Examples

Here are some life-directing dreams I've had.

Fashion Coordinator
Several years ago I dreamed that I was a Fashion Coordinator for a new store in the town where I was living. I'd been looking for a job in the natural and wanted desperately to work in a field that I would enjoy. I really loved Fashion, but had no idea how to enter the field in a mid-sized East Texas city.

The dream showed me going into a new store and telling someone inside it that I wanted to be Fashion Coordinator. They accepted me and I took the job.

Now, I don't have many literal dreams, but I do have seasons where my dreams are exceptionally literal. I even recalled the exact dress I'd worn into the store, which was in my closet. One of the ways you'll know when your dreams are for a current season or present day is that there will be clues in the dream that mark a particular time or season. In other words, yes, I owned that very dress right then, and I was really looking for a job.

When I woke that morning, I put on the dress I wore in the dream. What else was I going to do, right? I got into my car and drove directly to the newest department store in town. The store wasn't yet completed; the only accessible rooms were management offices. I marched in and told them the reason for my visit. The receptionist seemed startled and asked me to wait a moment. She called the General Merchandising Manager and let him know I was there.

He quizzically emerged from the back offices, asking how I knew that they were looking to add a Fashion Coordinator to their new staff. They hadn't yet run an ad for the position. They hadn't even announced publicly that anything like this was in the works for their new culture.

I think I merely smiled and shrugged my shoulders, not really knowing how to answer. He inquired as to whether I could interview models, hire models, train models and produce informal fashion shows in local restaurants every day in January!!! This, he said, was part of the Grand Opening campaign they had already planned! And of course my answer was, YES!

I started the job the following week! Those thirty days of Fashion Shows prepared me for the coming larger productions, and so on and so on...

This experience became my boot camp into the Fashion Industry, where I spent many years, loving every minute of it. I went on to take modeling prospects to New York City to meet with the major modeling agencies.
Needless to say, I wouldn't have wanted to miss that important dream message! It held the key to the next ten plus years of my life!

A Call From Sol

I worked in a furniture store some years ago after going back to school to work in Interior Design. One morning I dreamed that I was scheduled to be the first one in and open the store. When I got inside, the phone was already ringing. The office staff wasn't in yet, so I ran to answer it. It was a gentleman named Sol, who said he and his wife had been in the store the previous weekend and I showed them around. He said that he liked my enthusiasm and was impressed by my presentation. He asked me to join him and his wife for coffee to discuss going to work for them. As he was speaking, there was static on the line and it was difficult to understand everything he was saying. I woke thinking, "Huh, that was weird."

After waking, I dressed and drove to work. I had forgotten about the dream by then and my mind was on my day— right up until I unlocked the door of the store and heard the phone ringing. I ran in, grabbed the phone and answered. The voice was male. He asked if he was speaking with Melody. I answered, Yes, you are." He spoke every word from the dream phone call, telling me his name was Sol. Then he asked if I would be willing to have coffee with him and his wife to discuss going to work for them. I told him that I would have to get back with him and I took his number down.

Later I was thinking about the call and —just as in the dream, there was static on the line. I asked The Spirit under my breath what this was about, and quickly got an answer. What He said was this, "A message from Me will be clear, not full of static."

The next day I called and declined coffee with Sol and his wife. I did it out of obedience, but I couldn't help wondering how it would have turned out. A few weeks later I ran into a designer friend I hadn't seen in a while. I asked how she was and what she was doing.

She responded with disgust, saying she had gone to work for a specific company, thinking that it would be an opportunity for more freedom and creativity than her last job. She shared that her disgust was over not receiving pay for the six months she worked for them. As she spoke, I realized that Sol was the owner of the company! I felt terrible for her, but I must admit that I departed with a deeply grateful heart.

I had been protected from struggling for an income that would have been due me. <u>This</u> was another critical message for my life and circumstances.

<u>Warrior Mimi—Recurring Dream</u>

These dreams came to me at various ages: around 25, again at 30-something and later in my early 40's during crucial moments in my life—not that I was paying attention at these times, mind you!
The dream was exactly the same all three times I had it.

I woke from a dream within a dream. I heard turmoil outside the front of my family's home. Curious, I went to open the door and looked out. It was dark outside, still the wee hours of the night. My Grandmother (a sweet little denominational preacher's wife who probably never made any sort of fuss in her whole life/deceased) was standing facing North. I was acutely aware that the direction she faced was North.

Note: North can be connected to judgment against wickedness and also holds our spiritual inheritance, our identity. (True North) The number three is often related to something that is firmly established.

*She stood with strong resolve, almost in what I sensed was anger. I had NEVER seen my Mimi angry. I watched as she repeatedly lifted her arms toward the North, fervently calling something forth—**commanding** something or someone. I had no idea what she was doing.*

*Immediately in front of her was a small campfire; its embers floated into the air in front of her as though they were living beings. I couldn't catch what she was saying, but I knew she meant business. At some point she realized that I was there and she acknowledged me by pointing her right index finger directly at me and saying, "**Hear this Melody—this is about warfare!**" with a stern resolve in her voice.*

Her voice carried an authority I had never heard. The resonance of her sound emanated truth and resolve. I knew that what she was doing and saying was righteous and called for. It actually frightened me.

I stood paralyzed at the door soaking in the event—and then the scene changed. In the next scene I was going from room to room in my family home with all my family members standing next to or behind me. I was commanding as she had done. I was commanding curses to leave every room of the house. I spoke with the same authority she had used and, to my surprise, when I woke I knew something very critical had happened. I could feel the weight of some form of change coming. Little did I know that—just as Mimi had said— I would experience much more warfare in the coming years. This was the day my training began.

It was years later that I realized Creator was calling me to be militant in a few strategic areas: militant in breaking family curses, militant in standing in the spirit for and with my family, and militant in commanding the generational blessings and inheritance that were due me to come forth.

Before this happened, I had always been somewhat lackadaisical in nature. To this day I think of this dream and recall the truth that there is a rich heritage that Creator ordained for me. And to this day, I contend for what is rightfully mine in the spirit.

This dream opened my eyes to see important spiritual events taking place in the heavens and in realms outside the natural. This was an urgent destiny dream. It was a clarion call to stand in my true identity and destiny, to stand firmly in the radical realms I was created for.

Helpful Tips
(Getting Started)

1. Keep a journal and pen next to your bed
2. Consider sleeping with a mask and earplugs
3. Mentally recount the dream **before** turning on the light
4. Turn on a small dim light. (A book light is great.)
5. Write names, numbers and places down immediately
6. Take down main points before writing secondary details
7. Fill in the details last

Dream Template

In working with the template, give yourself a lot of grace. It's a great starting point. There are elements that should work for you, but don't worry about the ones that don't. I have included a place to record Volume # and Month/Year on the spine (permanent marker works best). This will help you organize important timelines and more easily reference previous dreams and their messages.

I refer to my dreams regularly so I don't neglect necessary actions and responses. **The way you respond to your dreams will often affect the course of your life.**

FYI: *Point of Reference* for me is usually something happening in the moment and in the natural, something that relates clearly to or could be related to the dream. *Connecting References/Notes* are something I often add later. In other words, I may dream about getting the book ready, not realizing that it's <u>this</u> very book the dream is about. I add the related notes to make my timeline or events work in connection with the dream. As the dots begin to connect, it all becomes clear.

The *Digital Time* often represents the location of a Bible verse, which gives me needed confirmation. Other times, it is a sound frequency or something kindred from the Lexicon/Concordance.

Google is your friend when it comes to dream research, especially with name meanings. Make good use of your resources. You might find a word of witness or further direction that you've been searching for.

Template Example

Day/Date: *Monday, December 30, 2012*
Digital Time: *1:58 am*
Emotion: *Urgency/Concern about being behind schedule*
Who: *Me only*
Where: *Nondescript*
When: *At present in dream/now*
What: *Editing Dream Journal*
Location of dream: *My kid's home*
Point of Reference: Title: *Trouble Publishing*
Scene # 1 Content:
I had the Dream Journal written and organized. It was ready to publish, but I was having difficulty uploading to send. I was concerned that I wouldn't make my deadline.

Connecting References/Notes:
I am in the midst of trying to get the Dream Journal completed. I have had some difficulty getting it edited and ready for publication. I have had to make several minor changes, but it has taken time and effort and has put me a bit behind.

Interpretation:
*In this case, the Connecting Reference/Notes **are** the interpretation. This was a literal dream.*

Daily Template

Day/Date: _____

Digital Time: _____

Emotion: _____

Who: _____

Where: _____

When: _____

What: _____

Location of Dream: _____

Point of Reference: _____

Title: _____

Scene # _____ Content:

_____
_____
_____
_____
_____
_____
_____
_____
_____
_____
_____
_____
_____
_____
_____
_____
_____
_____
_____
_____
_____
_____
_____
_____
_____
_____
_____
_____

Extra Room

_____
_____
_____
_____
_____
_____
_____
_____
_____
_____
_____
_____
_____
_____
_____
_____
_____
_____
_____
_____
_____
_____
_____

Connecting References/Notes:

_____
_____
_____

Interpretation:

_____
_____
_____
_____

Daily Template

Day/Date: _____

Digital Time: _____

Emotion: _____

Who: _____

Where: _____

When: _____

What: _____

Location of Dream: _____

Point of Reference: _____

Title: _____

Scene # _____ Content:

_____

_____

_____

_____

_____

_____

_____

_____

_____

_____

_____

_____

_____

_____

_____

_____

_____

_____

_____

_____

_____

_____

_____

_____

_____

_____

_____

_____

Extra Room

_____
_____
_____
_____
_____
_____
_____
_____
_____
_____
_____
_____
_____
_____
_____
_____
_____
_____
_____
_____
_____
_____
_____
_____
_____
_____
_____

Connecting References/Notes:

_____
_____
_____

Interpretation:

_____
_____
_____
_____

Daily Template

Day/Date: _____

Digital Time: _____

Emotion: _____

Who: _____

Where: _____

When: _____

What: _____

Location of Dream: _____

Point of Reference: _____

Title: _____

Scene # _____ Content:

_____

_____

_____

_____

_____

_____

_____

_____

_____

_____

_____

_____

_____

_____

_____

_____

_____

_____

_____

_____

_____

_____

_____

_____

_____

_____

_____

_____

Extra Room

_____
_____
_____
_____
_____
_____
_____
_____
_____
_____
_____
_____
_____
_____
_____
_____
_____
_____
_____
_____
_____
_____
_____
_____
_____
_____
_____

Connecting References/Notes:

_____
_____
_____

Interpretation:

_____
_____
_____

Daily Template

Day/Date: _____

Digital Time: _____

Emotion: _____

Who: _____

Where: _____

When: _____

What: _____

Location of Dream: _____

Point of Reference: _____

Title: _____

Scene # _____ Content:

_____

_____

_____

_____

_____

_____

_____

_____

_____

_____

_____

_____

_____

_____

_____

_____

_____

_____

_____

_____

_____

_____

_____

_____

_____

_____

_____

_____

Extra Room

_____
_____
_____
_____
_____
_____
_____
_____
_____
_____
_____
_____
_____
_____
_____
_____
_____
_____
_____
_____
_____
_____
_____
_____
_____
_____
_____
_____
_____
_____

Connecting References/Notes:

_____
_____
_____

Interpretation:

_____
_____
_____
_____

Daily Template

Day/Date: _____

Digital Time: _____

Emotion: _____

Who: _____

Where: _____

When: _____

What: _____

Location of Dream: _____

Point of Reference: _____

Title: _____

Scene # _____ Content:

_____
_____
_____
_____
_____
_____
_____
_____
_____
_____
_____
_____
_____
_____
_____
_____
_____
_____
_____
_____
_____
_____
_____
_____
_____
_____

Extra Room

_____
_____
_____
_____
_____
_____
_____
_____
_____
_____
_____
_____
_____
_____
_____
_____
_____
_____
_____
_____
_____
_____
_____
_____
_____
_____
_____

Connecting References/Notes:

_____
_____
_____

Interpretation:

_____
_____
_____
_____

Daily Template

Day/Date: _____

Digital Time: _____

Emotion: _____

Who: _____

Where: _____

When: _____

What: _____

Location of Dream: _____

Point of Reference: _____

Title: _____

Scene # _____ Content:

_____

_____

_____

_____

_____

_____

_____

_____

_____

_____

_____

_____

_____

_____

_____

_____

_____

_____

_____

_____

_____

_____

_____

_____

_____

_____

_____

_____

_____

_____

Extra Room

_____
_____
_____
_____
_____
_____
_____
_____
_____
_____
_____
_____
_____
_____
_____
_____
_____
_____
_____
_____
_____
_____
_____
_____
_____
_____
_____

Connecting References/Notes:

_____
_____
_____

Interpretation:

_____
_____
_____
_____

Daily Template

Day/Date: _____

Digital Time: _____

Emotion: _____

Who: _____

Where: _____

When: _____

What: _____

Location of Dream: _____

Point of Reference: _____

Title: _____

Scene # ____ Content:

_____

_____

_____

_____

_____

_____

_____

_____

_____

_____

_____

_____

_____

_____

_____

_____

_____

_____

_____

_____

_____

_____

_____

_____

_____

_____

_____

_____

_____

_____

_____

_____

Extra Room

_____
_____
_____
_____
_____
_____
_____
_____
_____
_____
_____
_____
_____
_____
_____
_____
_____
_____
_____
_____
_____
_____
_____
_____

Connecting References/Notes:

_____
_____
_____

Interpretation:

_____
_____
_____

Daily Template

Day/Date: _____

Digital Time: _____

Emotion: _____

Who: _____

Where: _____

When: _____

What: _____

Location of Dream: _____

Point of Reference: _____

Title: _____

Scene # _____ Content:

_____

_____

_____

_____

_____

_____

_____

_____

_____

_____

_____

_____

_____

_____

_____

_____

_____

_____

_____

_____

_____

_____

_____

_____

_____

_____

_____

_____

_____

Extra Room

_____
_____
_____
_____
_____
_____
_____
_____
_____
_____
_____
_____
_____
_____
_____
_____
_____
_____
_____
_____
_____
_____
_____
_____
_____

Connecting References/Notes:

_____
_____
_____

Interpretation:

_____
_____
_____

Daily Template

Day/Date: _____

Digital Time: _____

Emotion: _____

Who: _____

Where: _____

When: _____

What: _____

Location of Dream: _____

Point of Reference: _____

Title: _____

Scene # _____ Content:

_____

_____

_____

_____

_____

_____

_____

_____

_____

_____

_____

_____

_____

_____

_____

_____

_____

_____

_____

_____

_____

_____

_____

_____

_____

_____

_____

_____

Extra Room

_____
_____
_____
_____
_____
_____
_____
_____
_____
_____
_____
_____
_____
_____
_____
_____
_____
_____
_____
_____
_____
_____
_____
_____
_____
_____

Connecting References/Notes:

_____
_____
_____

Interpretation:

_____
_____
_____

Daily Template

Day/Date: _____

Digital Time: _____

Emotion: _____

Who: _____

Where: _____

When: _____

What: _____

Location of Dream: _____

Point of Reference: _____

Title: _____

Scene # _____ Content:

_____
_____
_____
_____
_____
_____
_____
_____
_____
_____
_____
_____
_____
_____
_____
_____
_____
_____
_____
_____
_____
_____
_____
_____
_____
_____
_____
_____

Extra Room

_____
_____
_____
_____
_____
_____
_____
_____
_____
_____
_____
_____
_____
_____
_____
_____
_____
_____
_____
_____
_____
_____
_____
_____
_____
_____

Connecting References/Notes:

_____
_____
_____

Interpretation:

_____
_____
_____

Daily Template

Day/Date: _____

Digital Time: _____

Emotion: _____

Who: _____

Where: _____

When: _____

What: _____

Location of Dream: _____

Point of Reference: _____

Title: _____

Scene # _____ Content:

_____

_____

_____

_____

_____

_____

_____

_____

_____

_____

_____

_____

_____

_____

_____

_____

_____

_____

_____

_____

_____

_____

_____

_____

_____

_____

_____

_____

_____

_____

_____

_____

Extra Room

_____
_____
_____
_____
_____
_____
_____
_____
_____
_____
_____
_____
_____
_____
_____
_____
_____
_____
_____
_____
_____
_____
_____
_____
_____

Connecting References/Notes:

_____
_____
_____

Interpretation:

_____
_____
_____

Daily Template

Day/Date: _____

Digital Time: _____

Emotion: _____

Who: _____

Where: _____

When: _____

What: _____

Location of Dream: _____

Point of Reference: _____

Title: _____

Scene # _____ Content:

_____

_____

_____

_____

_____

_____

_____

_____

_____

_____

_____

_____

_____

_____

_____

_____

_____

_____

_____

_____

_____

_____

_____

_____

_____

_____

_____

_____

_____

Extra Room

_____

_____

_____

_____

_____

_____

_____

_____

_____

_____

_____

_____

_____

_____

_____

_____

_____

_____

_____

_____

_____

_____

_____

_____

_____

_____

_____

_____

Connecting References/Notes:

_____

_____

_____

Interpretation:

_____

_____

_____

_____

Daily Template

Day/Date: _____

Digital Time: _____

Emotion: _____

Who: _____

Where: _____

When: _____

What: _____

Location of Dream: _____

Point of Reference: _____

Title: _____

Scene # _____ Content:

_____
_____
_____
_____
_____
_____
_____
_____
_____
_____
_____
_____
_____
_____
_____
_____
_____
_____
_____
_____
_____
_____
_____
_____
_____
_____
_____
_____

Extra Room

_____
_____
_____
_____
_____
_____
_____
_____
_____
_____
_____
_____
_____
_____
_____
_____
_____
_____
_____
_____
_____
_____
_____
_____
_____

Connecting References/Notes:

_____
_____
_____

Interpretation:

_____
_____
_____
_____

Daily Template

Day/Date: _____

Digital Time: _____

Emotion: _____

Who: _____

Where: _____

When: _____

What: _____

Location of Dream: _____

Point of Reference: _____

Title: _____

Scene # _____ Content:

_____

_____

_____

_____

_____

_____

_____

_____

_____

_____

_____

_____

_____

_____

_____

_____

_____

_____

_____

_____

_____

_____

_____

_____

_____

_____

_____

_____

_____

_____

Extra Room

_____

_____

_____

_____

_____

_____

_____

_____

_____

_____

_____

_____

_____

_____

_____

_____

_____

_____

_____

_____

_____

_____

_____

_____

_____

_____

_____

_____

_____

Connecting References/Notes:

_____

_____

_____

Interpretation:

_____

_____

_____

_____

Daily Template

Day/Date: _____

Digital Time: _____

Emotion: _____

Who: _____

Where: _____

When: _____

What: _____

Location of Dream: _____

Point of Reference: _____

Title: _____

Scene # _____ Content:

_____

_____

_____

_____

_____

_____

_____

_____

_____

_____

_____

_____

_____

_____

_____

_____

_____

_____

_____

_____

_____

_____

_____

_____

_____

_____

_____

_____

Extra Room

Connecting References/Notes:

Interpretation:

Daily Template

Day/Date: _____

Digital Time: _____

Emotion: _____

Who: _____

Where: _____

When: _____

What: _____

Location of Dream: _____

Point of Reference: _____

Title: _____

Scene # _____ Content:

_____

_____

_____

_____

_____

_____

_____

_____

_____

_____

_____

_____

_____

_____

_____

_____

_____

_____

_____

_____

_____

_____

_____

_____

_____

_____

_____

_____

_____

_____

Extra Room

_____
_____
_____
_____
_____
_____
_____
_____
_____
_____
_____
_____
_____
_____
_____
_____
_____
_____
_____
_____
_____
_____
_____
_____
_____

Connecting References/Notes:

_____
_____
_____

Interpretation:

_____
_____
_____

Daily Template

Day/Date: _____

Digital Time: _____

Emotion: _____

Who: _____

Where: _____

When: _____

What: _____

Location of Dream: _____

Point of Reference: _____

Title: _____

Scene # _____ Content:

_____

_____

_____

_____

_____

_____

_____

_____

_____

_____

_____

_____

_____

_____

_____

_____

_____

_____

_____

_____

_____

_____

_____

_____

_____

_____

_____

_____

Extra Room

_____
_____
_____
_____
_____
_____
_____
_____
_____
_____
_____
_____
_____
_____
_____
_____
_____
_____
_____
_____
_____
_____
_____
_____
_____

Connecting References/Notes:

_____
_____
_____

Interpretation:

_____
_____
_____
_____

Daily Template

Day/Date: _____

Digital Time: _____

Emotion: _____

Who: _____

Where: _____

When: _____

What: _____

Location of Dream: _____

Point of Reference: _____

Title: _____

Scene # _____ Content:

_____

_____

_____

_____

_____

_____

_____

_____

_____

_____

_____

_____

_____

_____

_____

_____

_____

_____

_____

_____

_____

_____

_____

_____

_____

_____

_____

_____

Extra Room

_____
_____
_____
_____
_____
_____
_____
_____
_____
_____
_____
_____
_____
_____
_____
_____
_____
_____
_____
_____
_____
_____
_____
_____
_____

Connecting References/Notes:

_____
_____
_____

Interpretation:

_____
_____
_____

Daily Template

Day/Date: _____

Digital Time: _____

Emotion: _____

Who: _____

Where: _____

When: _____

What: _____

Location of Dream: _____

Point of Reference: _____

Title: _____

Scene # _____ Content:

_____

_____

_____

_____

_____

_____

_____

_____

_____

_____

_____

_____

_____

_____

_____

_____

_____

_____

_____

_____

_____

_____

_____

_____

_____

_____

_____

Extra Room

_____
_____
_____
_____
_____
_____
_____
_____
_____
_____
_____
_____
_____
_____
_____
_____
_____
_____
_____
_____
_____
_____
_____
_____
_____
_____

Connecting References/Notes:

_____
_____
_____

Interpretation:

_____
_____
_____

Daily Template

Day/Date: _____

Digital Time: _____

Emotion: _____

Who: _____

Where: _____

When: _____

What: _____

Location of Dream: _____

Point of Reference: _____

Title: _____

Scene # _____ Content:

_____

_____

_____

_____

_____

_____

_____

_____

_____

_____

_____

_____

_____

_____

_____

_____

_____

_____

_____

_____

_____

_____

_____

_____

_____

_____

_____

_____

_____

Extra Room

_____
_____
_____
_____
_____
_____
_____
_____
_____
_____
_____
_____
_____
_____
_____
_____
_____
_____
_____
_____
_____
_____
_____
_____
_____
_____

Connecting References/Notes:

_____
_____
_____

Interpretation:

_____
_____
_____

Daily Template

Day/Date: _____

Digital Time: _____

Emotion: _____

Who: _____

Where: _____

When: _____

What: _____

Location of Dream: _____

Point of Reference: _____

Title: _____

Scene # _____ Content:

_____

_____

_____

_____

_____

_____

_____

_____

_____

_____

_____

_____

_____

_____

_____

_____

_____

_____

_____

_____

_____

_____

_____

_____

_____

_____

_____

_____

_____

Extra Room

_____
_____
_____
_____
_____
_____
_____
_____
_____
_____
_____
_____
_____
_____
_____
_____
_____
_____
_____
_____
_____
_____
_____
_____
_____
_____
_____
_____

Connecting References/Notes:

_____
_____
_____

Interpretation:

_____
_____
_____

Daily Template

Day/Date: _____

Digital Time: _____

Emotion: _____

Who: _____

Where: _____

When: _____

What: _____

Location of Dream: _____

Point of Reference: _____

Title: _____

Scene # _____ Content:

_____

_____

_____

_____

_____

_____

_____

_____

_____

_____

_____

_____

_____

_____

_____

_____

_____

_____

_____

_____

_____

_____

_____

_____

_____

_____

_____

_____

_____

_____

Extra Room

Connecting References/Notes:

Interpretation:

Daily Template

Day/Date: _____

Digital Time: _____

Emotion: _____

Who: _____

Where: _____

When: _____

What: _____

Location of Dream: _____

Point of Reference: _____

Title: _____

Scene # ____ Content:

_____

_____

_____

_____

_____

_____

_____

_____

_____

_____

_____

_____

_____

_____

_____

_____

_____

_____

_____

_____

_____

_____

_____

_____

_____

_____

_____

_____

_____

_____

Extra Room

_____
_____
_____
_____
_____
_____
_____
_____
_____
_____
_____
_____
_____
_____
_____
_____
_____
_____
_____
_____
_____
_____
_____
_____
_____
_____
_____
_____

Connecting References/Notes:

_____
_____
_____

Interpretation:

_____
_____
_____
_____

Daily Template

Day/Date: _____

Digital Time: _____

Emotion: _____

Who: _____

Where: _____

When: _____

What: _____

Location of Dream: _____

Point of Reference: _____

Title: _____

Scene # _____ Content:

_____
_____
_____
_____
_____
_____
_____
_____
_____
_____
_____
_____
_____
_____
_____
_____
_____
_____
_____
_____
_____
_____
_____
_____
_____
_____
_____
_____

Extra Room

Connecting References/Notes:

Interpretation:

Daily Template

Day/Date: _____

Digital Time: _____

Emotion: _____

Who: _____

Where: _____

When: _____

What: _____

Location of Dream: _____

Point of Reference: _____

Title: _____

Scene # _____ Content:

_____
_____
_____
_____
_____
_____
_____
_____
_____
_____
_____
_____
_____
_____
_____
_____
_____
_____
_____
_____
_____
_____
_____
_____
_____
_____
_____
_____

Extra Room

_____
_____
_____
_____
_____
_____
_____
_____
_____
_____
_____
_____
_____
_____
_____
_____
_____
_____
_____
_____
_____
_____
_____
_____
_____
_____

Connecting References/Notes:

_____
_____
_____

Interpretation:

_____
_____
_____
_____

Daily Template

Day/Date: _____

Digital Time: _____

Emotion: _____

Who: _____

Where: _____

When: _____

What: _____

Location of Dream: _____

Point of Reference: _____

Title: _____

Scene # _____ Content:

_____
_____
_____
_____
_____
_____
_____
_____
_____
_____
_____
_____
_____
_____
_____
_____
_____
_____
_____
_____
_____
_____
_____
_____
_____
_____
_____
_____

Extra Room

_____
_____
_____
_____
_____
_____
_____
_____
_____
_____
_____
_____
_____
_____
_____
_____
_____
_____
_____
_____
_____
_____
_____

Connecting References/Notes:

_____
_____
_____

Interpretation:

_____
_____
_____
_____

Daily Template

Day/Date: _____

Digital Time: _____

Emotion: _____

Who: _____

Where: _____

When: _____

What: _____

Location of Dream: _____

Point of Reference: _____

Title: _____

Scene # _____ Content:

_____
_____
_____
_____
_____
_____
_____
_____
_____
_____
_____
_____
_____
_____
_____
_____
_____
_____
_____
_____
_____
_____
_____
_____
_____
_____
_____
_____

Extra Room

_____
_____
_____
_____
_____
_____
_____
_____
_____
_____
_____
_____
_____
_____
_____
_____
_____
_____
_____
_____
_____
_____
_____
_____
_____

Connecting References/Notes:

_____
_____
_____

Interpretation:

_____
_____
_____
_____

Daily Template

Day/Date: _____

Digital Time: _____

Emotion: _____

Who: _____

Where: _____

When: _____

What: _____

Location of Dream: _____

Point of Reference: _____

Title: _____

Scene # _____ Content:

_____
_____
_____
_____
_____
_____
_____
_____
_____
_____
_____
_____
_____
_____
_____
_____
_____
_____
_____
_____
_____
_____
_____
_____
_____
_____
_____

Extra Room

_____
_____
_____
_____
_____
_____
_____
_____
_____
_____
_____
_____
_____
_____
_____
_____
_____
_____
_____
_____
_____
_____
_____
_____

Connecting References/Notes:

_____
_____
_____

Interpretation:

_____
_____
_____
_____

Daily Template

Day/Date: _____

Digital Time: _____

Emotion: _____

Who: _____

Where: _____

When: _____

What: _____

Location of Dream: _____

Point of Reference: _____

Title: _____

Scene # _____ Content:

_____

_____

_____

_____

_____

_____

_____

_____

_____

_____

_____

_____

_____

_____

_____

_____

_____

_____

_____

_____

_____

_____

_____

_____

_____

_____

_____

_____

_____

_____

Extra Room

_____

Connecting References/Notes:

_____

Interpretation:

_____

Daily Template

Day/Date: _____

Digital Time: _____

Emotion: _____

Who: _____

Where: _____

When: _____

What: _____

Location of Dream: _____

Point of Reference: _____

Title: _____

Scene # _____ Content:

_____
_____
_____
_____
_____
_____
_____
_____
_____
_____
_____
_____
_____
_____
_____
_____
_____
_____
_____
_____
_____
_____
_____
_____
_____
_____
_____
_____

Extra Room

_____
_____
_____
_____
_____
_____
_____
_____
_____
_____
_____
_____
_____
_____
_____
_____
_____
_____
_____
_____
_____
_____
_____
_____
_____
_____
_____
_____

Connecting References/Notes:

_____
_____
_____

Interpretation:

_____
_____
_____
_____

Daily Template

Day/Date: _____

Digital Time: _____

Emotion: _____

Who: _____

Where: _____

When: _____

What: _____

Location of Dream: _____

Point of Reference: _____

Title: _____

Scene # _____ Content:

_____

_____

_____

_____

_____

_____

_____

_____

_____

_____

_____

_____

_____

_____

_____

_____

_____

_____

_____

_____

_____

_____

_____

_____

_____

_____

_____

_____

Extra Room

_____
_____
_____
_____
_____
_____
_____
_____
_____
_____
_____
_____
_____
_____
_____
_____
_____
_____
_____
_____
_____
_____
_____
_____
_____

Connecting References/Notes:

_____
_____
_____

Interpretation:

_____
_____
_____
_____

Daily Template

Day/Date: _____

Digital Time: _____

Emotion: _____

Who: _____

Where: _____

When: _____

What: _____

Location of Dream: _____

Point of Reference: _____

Title: _____

Scene # _____ Content:

_____

_____

_____

_____

_____

_____

_____

_____

_____

_____

_____

_____

_____

_____

_____

_____

_____

_____

_____

_____

_____

_____

_____

_____

_____

_____

Extra Room

_____
_____
_____
_____
_____
_____
_____
_____
_____
_____
_____
_____
_____
_____
_____
_____
_____
_____
_____
_____
_____
_____
_____
_____
_____

Connecting References/Notes:

_____
_____
_____

Interpretation:

_____
_____
_____
_____

Daily Template

Day/Date: _____

Digital Time: _____

Emotion: _____

Who: _____

Where: _____

When: _____

What: _____

Location of Dream: _____

Point of Reference: _____

Title: _____

Scene # _____ Content:

_____

_____

_____

_____

_____

_____

_____

_____

_____

_____

_____

_____

_____

_____

_____

_____

_____

_____

_____

_____

_____

_____

_____

_____

_____

_____

_____

_____

_____

_____

Extra Room

_____

Connecting References/Notes:

_____

Interpretation:

_____

Daily Template

Day/Date: _____

Digital Time: _____

Emotion: _____

Who: _____

Where: _____

When: _____

What: _____

Location of Dream: _____

Point of Reference: _____

Title: _____

Scene # _____ Content:

_____

_____

_____

_____

_____

_____

_____

_____

_____

_____

_____

_____

_____

_____

_____

_____

_____

_____

_____

_____

_____

_____

_____

_____

_____

_____

_____

Extra Room

_____
_____
_____
_____
_____
_____
_____
_____
_____
_____
_____
_____
_____
_____
_____
_____
_____
_____
_____
_____
_____
_____
_____

Connecting References/Notes:

_____
_____
_____

Interpretation:

_____
_____
_____

Daily Template

Day/Date: _____

Digital Time: _____

Emotion: _____

Who: _____

Where: _____

When: _____

What: _____

Location of Dream: _____

Point of Reference: _____

Title: _____

Scene # _____ Content:

_____

_____

_____

_____

_____

_____

_____

_____

_____

_____

_____

_____

_____

_____

_____

_____

_____

_____

_____

_____

_____

_____

_____

_____

_____

_____

_____

_____

_____

Extra Room

_____
_____
_____
_____
_____
_____
_____
_____
_____
_____
_____
_____
_____
_____
_____
_____
_____
_____
_____
_____
_____
_____
_____
_____
_____

Connecting References/Notes:

_____
_____
_____

Interpretation:

_____
_____
_____

Daily Template

Day/Date: _____

Digital Time: _____

Emotion: _____

Who: _____

Where: _____

When: _____

What: _____

Location of Dream: _____

Point of Reference: _____

Title: _____

Scene # _____ Content:

_____

_____

_____

_____

_____

_____

_____

_____

_____

_____

_____

_____

_____

_____

_____

_____

_____

_____

_____

_____

_____

_____

_____

_____

_____

_____

_____

_____

Extra Room

_____

_____

_____

_____

_____

_____

_____

_____

_____

_____

_____

_____

_____

_____

_____

_____

_____

_____

_____

_____

_____

_____

_____

_____

_____

_____

_____

Connecting References/Notes:

_____

_____

_____

Interpretation:

_____

_____

_____

Daily Template

Day/Date: _____

Digital Time: _____

Emotion: _____

Who: _____

Where: _____

When: _____

What: _____

Location of Dream: _____

Point of Reference: _____

Title: _____

Scene # _____ Content:

_____
_____
_____
_____
_____
_____
_____
_____
_____
_____
_____
_____
_____
_____
_____
_____
_____
_____
_____
_____
_____
_____
_____
_____
_____
_____
_____

Extra Room

_____
_____
_____
_____
_____
_____
_____
_____
_____
_____
_____
_____
_____
_____
_____
_____
_____
_____
_____
_____
_____
_____
_____
_____

Connecting References/Notes:

_____
_____
_____

Interpretation:

_____
_____
_____
_____

Daily Template

Day/Date: _____

Digital Time: _____

Emotion: _____

Who: _____

Where: _____

When: _____

What: _____

Location of Dream: _____

Point of Reference: _____

Title: _____

Scene # _____ Content:

_____

_____

_____

_____

_____

_____

_____

_____

_____

_____

_____

_____

_____

_____

_____

_____

_____

_____

_____

_____

_____

_____

_____

_____

_____

_____

_____

_____

Extra Room

_____
_____
_____
_____
_____
_____
_____
_____
_____
_____
_____
_____
_____
_____
_____
_____
_____
_____
_____
_____
_____
_____
_____
_____
_____
_____
_____

Connecting References/Notes:

_____
_____
_____

Interpretation:

_____
_____
_____
_____

Daily Template

Day/Date: _____

Digital Time: _____

Emotion: _____

Who: _____

Where: _____

When: _____

What: _____

Location of Dream: _____

Point of Reference: _____

Title: _____

Scene # _____ Content:

_____
_____
_____
_____
_____
_____
_____
_____
_____
_____
_____
_____
_____
_____
_____
_____
_____
_____
_____
_____
_____
_____
_____
_____
_____
_____
_____

Extra Room

_____
_____
_____
_____
_____
_____
_____
_____
_____
_____
_____
_____
_____
_____
_____
_____
_____
_____
_____
_____
_____
_____
_____
_____
_____

Connecting References/Notes:

_____
_____
_____

Interpretation:

_____
_____
_____

Daily Template

Day/Date: _____

Digital Time: _____

Emotion: _____

Who: _____

Where: _____

When: _____

What: _____

Location of Dream: _____

Point of Reference: _____

Title: _____

Scene # _____ Content:

_____
_____
_____
_____
_____
_____
_____
_____
_____
_____
_____
_____
_____
_____
_____
_____
_____
_____
_____
_____
_____
_____
_____
_____
_____
_____
_____
_____

Extra Room

_____
_____
_____
_____
_____
_____
_____
_____
_____
_____
_____
_____
_____
_____
_____
_____
_____
_____
_____
_____
_____
_____
_____
_____
_____
_____
_____

Connecting References/Notes:

_____
_____
_____

Interpretation:

_____
_____
_____
_____

Daily Template

Day/Date: _____

Digital Time: _____

Emotion: _____

Who: _____

Where: _____

When: _____

What: _____

Location of Dream: _____

Point of Reference: _____

Title: _____

Scene # _____ Content:

_____

_____

_____

_____

_____

_____

_____

_____

_____

_____

_____

_____

_____

_____

_____

_____

_____

_____

_____

_____

_____

_____

_____

_____

_____

_____

_____

_____

_____

Extra Room

_____
_____
_____
_____
_____
_____
_____
_____
_____
_____
_____
_____
_____
_____
_____
_____
_____
_____
_____
_____
_____
_____
_____
_____
_____
_____

Connecting References/Notes:

_____
_____
_____

Interpretation:

_____
_____
_____
_____

Daily Template

Day/Date: _____

Digital Time: _____

Emotion: _____

Who: _____

Where: _____

When: _____

What: _____

Location of Dream: _____

Point of Reference: _____

Title: _____

Scene # _____ Content:

_____

_____

_____

_____

_____

_____

_____

_____

_____

_____

_____

_____

_____

_____

_____

_____

_____

_____

_____

_____

_____

_____

_____

_____

_____

_____

_____

_____

_____

_____

Extra Room

_____
_____
_____
_____
_____
_____
_____
_____
_____
_____
_____
_____
_____
_____
_____
_____
_____
_____
_____
_____
_____
_____
_____
_____
_____
_____
_____
_____
_____
_____

Connecting References/Notes:

_____
_____
_____

Interpretation:

_____
_____
_____
_____

Daily Template

Day/Date: _____

Digital Time: _____

Emotion: _____

Who: _____

Where: _____

When: _____

What: _____

Location of Dream: _____

Point of Reference: _____

Title: _____

Scene # _____ Content:

_____

_____

_____

_____

_____

_____

_____

_____

_____

_____

_____

_____

_____

_____

_____

_____

_____

_____

_____

_____

_____

_____

_____

_____

_____

_____

_____

_____

Extra Room

Connecting References/Notes:

Interpretation:

Daily Template

Day/Date: _____

Digital Time: _____

Emotion: _____

Who: _____

Where: _____

When: _____

What: _____

Location of Dream: _____

Point of Reference: _____

Title: _____

Scene # _____ Content:

_____
_____
_____
_____
_____
_____
_____
_____
_____
_____
_____
_____
_____
_____
_____
_____
_____
_____
_____
_____
_____
_____
_____
_____
_____
_____
_____
_____

Extra Room

_____
_____
_____
_____
_____
_____
_____
_____
_____
_____
_____
_____
_____
_____
_____
_____
_____
_____
_____
_____
_____
_____
_____
_____
_____
_____
_____
_____
_____
_____
_____
_____
_____

Connecting References/Notes:

_____
_____
_____

Interpretation:

_____
_____
_____
_____

Daily Template

Day/Date: _____

Digital Time: _____

Emotion: _____

Who: _____

Where: _____

When: _____

What: _____

Location of Dream: _____

Point of Reference: _____

Title: _____

Scene # _____ Content:

_____

_____

_____

_____

_____

_____

_____

_____

_____

_____

_____

_____

_____

_____

_____

_____

_____

_____

_____

_____

_____

_____

_____

_____

_____

_____

_____

_____

_____

Extra Room

Connecting References/Notes:

Interpretation:

Daily Template

Day/Date: _____

Digital Time: _____

Emotion: _____

Who: _____

Where: _____

When: _____

What: _____

Location of Dream: _____

Point of Reference: _____

Title: _____

Scene # _____ Content:

_____
_____
_____
_____
_____
_____
_____
_____
_____
_____
_____
_____
_____
_____
_____
_____
_____
_____
_____
_____
_____
_____
_____
_____
_____
_____
_____
_____

Extra Room

_____
_____
_____
_____
_____
_____
_____
_____
_____
_____
_____
_____
_____
_____
_____
_____
_____
_____
_____
_____
_____
_____
_____
_____
_____

Connecting References/Notes:

_____
_____
_____

Interpretation:

_____
_____
_____
_____

Daily Template

Day/Date: _____

Digital Time: _____

Emotion: _____

Who: _____

Where: _____

When: _____

What: _____

Location of Dream: _____

Point of Reference: _____

Title: _____

Scene # _____ Content:

_____

_____

_____

_____

_____

_____

_____

_____

_____

_____

_____

_____

_____

_____

_____

_____

_____

_____

_____

_____

_____

_____

_____

_____

_____

_____

_____

_____

_____

Extra Room

_____

_____

_____

_____

_____

_____

_____

_____

_____

_____

_____

_____

_____

_____

_____

_____

_____

_____

_____

_____

_____

_____

_____

_____

_____

Connecting References/Notes:

_____

_____

_____

Interpretation:

_____

_____

_____

_____

Daily Template

Day/Date: _____

Digital Time: _____

Emotion: _____

Who: _____

Where: _____

When: _____

What: _____

Location of Dream: _____

Point of Reference: _____

Title: _____

Scene # _____ Content:

_____

_____

_____

_____

_____

_____

_____

_____

_____

_____

_____

_____

_____

_____

_____

_____

_____

_____

_____

_____

_____

_____

_____

_____

_____

_____

_____

_____

_____

Extra Room

_____

Connecting References/Notes:

_____

Interpretation:

_____

Daily Template

Day/Date: _____

Digital Time: _____

Emotion: _____

Who: _____

Where: _____

When: _____

What: _____

Location of Dream: _____

Point of Reference: _____

Title: _____

Scene # _____ Content:

_____

_____

_____

_____

_____

_____

_____

_____

_____

_____

_____

_____

_____

_____

_____

_____

_____

_____

_____

_____

_____

_____

_____

_____

_____

_____

_____

Extra Room

Connecting References/Notes:

Interpretation:

Daily Template

Day/Date: _____

Digital Time: _____

Emotion: _____

Who: _____

Where: _____

When: _____

What: _____

Location of Dream: _____

Point of Reference: _____

Title: _____

Scene # _____ Content:

_____
_____
_____
_____
_____
_____
_____
_____
_____
_____
_____
_____
_____
_____
_____
_____
_____
_____
_____
_____
_____
_____
_____
_____
_____
_____

Extra Room

_____
_____
_____
_____
_____
_____
_____
_____
_____
_____
_____
_____
_____
_____
_____
_____
_____
_____
_____
_____
_____
_____
_____
_____
_____
_____
_____
_____

Connecting References/Notes:

_____
_____
_____

Interpretation:

_____
_____
_____

Daily Template

Day/Date: _____

Digital Time: _____

Emotion: _____

Who: _____

Where: _____

When: _____

What: _____

Location of Dream: _____

Point of Reference: _____

Title: _____

Scene # _____ Content:

_____
_____
_____
_____
_____
_____
_____
_____
_____
_____
_____
_____
_____
_____
_____
_____
_____
_____
_____
_____
_____
_____
_____
_____
_____
_____
_____
_____
_____

Extra Room

_____
_____
_____
_____
_____
_____
_____
_____
_____
_____
_____
_____
_____
_____
_____
_____
_____
_____
_____
_____
_____
_____
_____
_____
_____
_____
_____
_____

Connecting References/Notes:

_____
_____
_____

Interpretation:

_____
_____
_____

Daily Template

Day/Date: _____

Digital Time: _____

Emotion: _____

Who: _____

Where: _____

When: _____

What: _____

Location of Dream: _____

Point of Reference: _____

Title: _____

Scene # _____ Content:

_____
_____
_____
_____
_____
_____
_____
_____
_____
_____
_____
_____
_____
_____
_____
_____
_____
_____
_____
_____
_____
_____
_____
_____
_____
_____
_____
_____

Extra Room

Connecting References/Notes:

Interpretation:

Daily Template

Day/Date: _____

Digital Time: _____

Emotion: _____

Who: _____

Where: _____

When: _____

What: _____

Location of Dream: _____

Point of Reference: _____

Title: _____

Scene # _____ Content:

_____
_____
_____
_____
_____
_____
_____
_____
_____
_____
_____
_____
_____
_____
_____
_____
_____
_____
_____
_____
_____
_____
_____
_____
_____
_____
_____
_____
_____
_____

Extra Room

Connecting References/Notes:

Interpretation:

Daily Template

Day/Date: _____

Digital Time: _____

Emotion: _____

Who: _____

Where: _____

When: _____

What: _____

Location of Dream: _____

Point of Reference: _____

Title: _____

Scene # _____ Content:

_____

_____

_____

_____

_____

_____

_____

_____

_____

_____

_____

_____

_____

_____

_____

_____

_____

_____

_____

_____

_____

_____

_____

_____

_____

_____

_____

_____

Extra Room

Connecting References/Notes:

Interpretation:

Daily Template

Day/Date: _____

Digital Time: _____

Emotion: _____

Who: _____

Where: _____

When: _____

What: _____

Location of Dream: _____

Point of Reference: _____

Title: _____

Scene # _____ Content:

_____

_____

_____

_____

_____

_____

_____

_____

_____

_____

_____

_____

_____

_____

_____

_____

_____

_____

_____

_____

_____

_____

_____

_____

_____

_____

_____

_____

Extra Room

Connecting References/Notes:

Interpretation:

Daily Template

Day/Date: _____

Digital Time: _____

Emotion: _____

Who: _____

Where: _____

When: _____

What: _____

Location of Dream: _____

Point of Reference: _____

Title: _____

Scene # _____ Content:

_____
_____
_____
_____
_____
_____
_____
_____
_____
_____
_____
_____
_____
_____
_____
_____
_____
_____
_____
_____
_____
_____
_____
_____
_____
_____
_____
_____
_____
_____
_____

Extra Room

Connecting References/Notes:

Interpretation:

Daily Template

Day/Date: _____

Digital Time: _____

Emotion: _____

Who: _____

Where: _____

When: _____

What: _____

Location of Dream: _____

Point of Reference: _____

Title: _____

Scene # _____ Content:

_____

_____

_____

_____

_____

_____

_____

_____

_____

_____

_____

_____

_____

_____

_____

_____

_____

_____

_____

_____

_____

_____

_____

_____

_____

_____

_____

_____

Extra Room

Connecting References/Notes:

Interpretation:

Daily Template

Day/Date: _____

Digital Time: _____

Emotion: _____

Who: _____

Where: _____

When: _____

What: _____

Location of Dream: _____

Point of Reference: _____

Title: _____

Scene # _____ Content:

_____

_____

_____

_____

_____

_____

_____

_____

_____

_____

_____

_____

_____

_____

_____

_____

_____

_____

_____

_____

_____

_____

_____

_____

_____

_____

_____

_____

Extra Room

Connecting References/Notes:

Interpretation:

Daily Template

Day/Date: _____

Digital Time: _____

Emotion: _____

Who: _____

Where: _____

When: _____

What: _____

Location of Dream: _____

Point of Reference: _____

Title: _____

Scene # _____ Content:

_____
_____
_____
_____
_____
_____
_____
_____
_____
_____
_____
_____
_____
_____
_____
_____
_____
_____
_____
_____
_____
_____
_____
_____
_____
_____
_____
_____
_____

Extra Room

Connecting References/Notes:

Interpretation:

Daily Template

Day/Date: _____

Digital Time: _____

Emotion: _____

Who: _____

Where: _____

When: _____

What: _____

Location of Dream: _____

Point of Reference: _____

Title: _____

Scene # _____ Content:

_____

_____

_____

_____

_____

_____

_____

_____

_____

_____

_____

_____

_____

_____

_____

_____

_____

_____

_____

_____

_____

_____

_____

_____

_____

_____

_____

_____

_____

Extra Room

Connecting References/Notes:

Interpretation:

Daily Template

Day/Date: _____

Digital Time: _____

Emotion: _____

Who: _____

Where: _____

When: _____

What: _____

Location of Dream: _____

Point of Reference: _____

Title: _____

Scene # _____ Content:

_____

_____

_____

_____

_____

_____

_____

_____

_____

_____

_____

_____

_____

_____

_____

_____

_____

_____

_____

_____

_____

_____

_____

_____

_____

_____

_____

_____

_____

Extra Room

Connecting References/Notes:

Interpretation:

Daily Template

Day/Date: _____

Digital Time: _____

Emotion: _____

Who: _____

Where: _____

When: _____

What: _____

Location of Dream: _____

Point of Reference: _____

Title: _____

Scene # _____ Content:

_____
_____
_____
_____
_____
_____
_____
_____
_____
_____
_____
_____
_____
_____
_____
_____
_____
_____
_____
_____
_____
_____
_____
_____
_____
_____
_____
_____

Extra Room

Connecting References/Notes:

Interpretation:

Daily Template

Day/Date: _____

Digital Time: _____

Emotion: _____

Who: _____

Where: _____

When: _____

What: _____

Location of Dream: _____

Point of Reference: _____

Title: _____

Scene # _____ Content:

_____

_____

_____

_____

_____

_____

_____

_____

_____

_____

_____

_____

_____

_____

_____

_____

_____

_____

_____

_____

_____

_____

_____

_____

_____

_____

_____

_____

_____

_____

Extra Room

Connecting References/Notes:

Interpretation:

Daily Template

Day/Date: _____

Digital Time: _____

Emotion: _____

Who: _____

Where: _____

When: _____

What: _____

Location of Dream: _____

Point of Reference: _____

Title: _____

Scene # _____ Content:

_____
_____
_____
_____
_____
_____
_____
_____
_____
_____
_____
_____
_____
_____
_____
_____
_____
_____
_____
_____
_____
_____
_____
_____
_____
_____
_____
_____
_____

Extra Room

Connecting References/Notes:

Interpretation:

Daily Template

Day/Date: _____

Digital Time: _____

Emotion: _____

Who: _____

Where: _____

When: _____

What: _____

Location of Dream: _____

Point of Reference: _____

Title: _____

Scene # _____ Content:

_____
_____
_____
_____
_____
_____
_____
_____
_____
_____
_____
_____
_____
_____
_____
_____
_____
_____
_____
_____
_____
_____
_____
_____
_____
_____
_____

Extra Room

_____
_____
_____
_____
_____
_____
_____
_____
_____
_____
_____
_____
_____
_____
_____
_____
_____
_____
_____
_____
_____
_____
_____
_____
_____
_____

Connecting References/Notes:

_____
_____
_____

Interpretation:

_____
_____
_____
_____

Daily Template

Day/Date: _____

Digital Time: _____

Emotion: _____

Who: _____

Where: _____

When: _____

What: _____

Location of Dream: _____

Point of Reference: _____

Title: _____

Scene # _____ Content:

_____

_____

_____

_____

_____

_____

_____

_____

_____

_____

_____

_____

_____

_____

_____

_____

_____

_____

_____

_____

_____

_____

_____

_____

_____

_____

_____

_____

_____

_____

_____

_____

Extra Room

Connecting References/Notes:

Interpretation:

Daily Template

Day/Date: _____

Digital Time: _____

Emotion: _____

Who: _____

Where: _____

When: _____

What: _____

Location of Dream: _____

Point of Reference: _____

Title: _____

Scene # _____ Content:

_____

_____

_____

_____

_____

_____

_____

_____

_____

_____

_____

_____

_____

_____

_____

_____

_____

_____

_____

_____

_____

_____

_____

_____

_____

_____

_____

_____

Extra Room

Connecting References/Notes:

Interpretation:

Daily Template

Day/Date: _____

Digital Time: _____

Emotion: _____

Who: _____

Where: _____

When: _____

What: _____

Location of Dream: _____

Point of Reference: _____

Title: _____

Scene # _____ Content:

_____

_____

_____

_____

_____

_____

_____

_____

_____

_____

_____

_____

_____

_____

_____

_____

_____

_____

_____

_____

_____

_____

_____

_____

_____

_____

Extra Room

Connecting References/Notes:

Interpretation:

Daily Template

Day/Date: _____

Digital Time: _____

Emotion: _____

Who: _____

Where: _____

When: _____

What: _____

Location of Dream: _____

Point of Reference: _____

Title: _____

Scene # _____ Content:

_____

_____

_____

_____

_____

_____

_____

_____

_____

_____

_____

_____

_____

_____

_____

_____

_____

_____

_____

_____

_____

_____

_____

_____

_____

_____

_____

_____

Extra Room

Connecting References/Notes:

Interpretation:

Daily Template

Day/Date: _____

Digital Time: _____

Emotion: _____

Who: _____

Where: _____

When: _____

What: _____

Location of Dream: _____

Point of Reference: _____

Title: _____

Scene # _____ Content:

_____

_____

_____

_____

_____

_____

_____

_____

_____

_____

_____

_____

_____

_____

_____

_____

_____

_____

_____

_____

_____

_____

_____

_____

_____

_____

_____

Extra Room

Connecting References/Notes:

Interpretation:

Daily Template

Day/Date: _____

Digital Time: _____

Emotion: _____

Who: _____

Where: _____

When: _____

What: _____

Location of Dream: _____

Point of Reference: _____

Title: _____

Scene # _____ Content:

_____

_____

_____

_____

_____

_____

_____

_____

_____

_____

_____

_____

_____

_____

_____

_____

_____

_____

_____

_____

_____

_____

_____

_____

_____

Extra Room

_____

Connecting References/Notes:

_____

Interpretation:

_____

Daily Template

Day/Date: _____

Digital Time: _____

Emotion: _____

Who: _____

Where: _____

When: _____

What: _____

Location of Dream: _____

Point of Reference: _____

Title: _____

Scene # _____ Content:

_____

_____

_____

_____

_____

_____

_____

_____

_____

_____

_____

_____

_____

_____

_____

_____

_____

_____

_____

_____

_____

_____

_____

_____

_____

_____

_____

_____

Extra Room

Connecting References/Notes:

Interpretation:

Daily Template

Day/Date: _____

Digital Time: _____

Emotion: _____

Who: _____

Where: _____

When: _____

What: _____

Location of Dream: _____

Point of Reference: _____

Title: _____

Scene # _____ Content:

_____

_____

_____

_____

_____

_____

_____

_____

_____

_____

_____

_____

_____

_____

_____

_____

_____

_____

_____

_____

_____

_____

_____

_____

_____

_____

_____

_____

Extra Room

Connecting References/Notes:

Interpretation:

Daily Template

Day/Date: _____

Digital Time: _____

Emotion: _____

Who: _____

Where: _____

When: _____

What: _____

Location of Dream: _____

Point of Reference: _____

Title: _____

Scene # _____ Content:

_____
_____
_____
_____
_____
_____
_____
_____
_____
_____
_____
_____
_____
_____
_____
_____
_____
_____
_____
_____
_____
_____
_____
_____
_____

Extra Room

Connecting References/Notes:

Interpretation:

Daily Template

Day/Date: _____

Digital Time: _____

Emotion: _____

Who: _____

Where: _____

When: _____

What: _____

Location of Dream: _____

Point of Reference: _____

Title: _____

Scene # _____ Content:

_____
_____
_____
_____
_____
_____
_____
_____
_____
_____
_____
_____
_____
_____
_____
_____
_____
_____
_____
_____
_____
_____
_____
_____
_____
_____
_____

Extra Room

Connecting References/Notes:

Interpretation:

Daily Template

Day/Date: _____

Digital Time: _____

Emotion: _____

Who: _____

Where: _____

When: _____

What: _____

Location of Dream: _____

Point of Reference: _____

Title: _____

Scene # _____ Content:

_____
_____
_____
_____
_____
_____
_____
_____
_____
_____
_____
_____
_____
_____
_____
_____
_____
_____
_____
_____
_____
_____
_____
_____
_____
_____
_____
_____
_____
_____

Extra Room

_____
_____
_____
_____
_____
_____
_____
_____
_____
_____
_____
_____
_____
_____
_____
_____
_____
_____
_____
_____
_____
_____
_____

Connecting References/Notes:

_____
_____
_____

Interpretation:

_____
_____
_____

Daily Template

Day/Date: _____

Digital Time: _____

Emotion: _____

Who: _____

Where: _____

When: _____

What: _____

Location of Dream: _____

Point of Reference: _____

Title: _____

Scene # _____ Content:

_____

_____

_____

_____

_____

_____

_____

_____

_____

_____

_____

_____

_____

_____

_____

_____

_____

_____

_____

_____

_____

_____

_____

_____

_____

_____

_____

_____

_____

Extra Room

Connecting References/Notes:

Interpretation:

Daily Template

Day/Date: _____

Digital Time: _____

Emotion: _____

Who: _____

Where: _____

When: _____

What: _____

Location of Dream: _____

Point of Reference: _____

Title: _____

Scene # _____ Content:

_____

_____

_____

_____

_____

_____

_____

_____

_____

_____

_____

_____

_____

_____

_____

_____

_____

_____

_____

_____

_____

_____

_____

_____

_____

_____

_____

_____

Extra Room

Connecting References/Notes:

Interpretation:

Daily Template

Day/Date: _____

Digital Time: _____

Emotion: _____

Who: _____

Where: _____

When: _____

What: _____

Location of Dream: _____

Point of Reference: _____

Title: _____

Scene # _____ Content:

_____

_____

_____

_____

_____

_____

_____

_____

_____

_____

_____

_____

_____

_____

_____

_____

_____

_____

_____

_____

_____

_____

_____

_____

_____

_____

_____

_____

_____

_____

Extra Room

Connecting References/Notes:

Interpretation:

Daily Template

Day/Date: _____

Digital Time: _____

Emotion: _____

Who: _____

Where: _____

When: _____

What: _____

Location of Dream: _____

Point of Reference: _____

Title: _____

Scene # _____ Content:

_____

_____

_____

_____

_____

_____

_____

_____

_____

_____

_____

_____

_____

_____

_____

_____

_____

_____

_____

_____

_____

_____

_____

_____

_____

_____

_____

_____

_____

Extra Room

_____
_____
_____
_____
_____
_____
_____
_____
_____
_____
_____
_____
_____
_____
_____
_____
_____
_____
_____
_____
_____
_____
_____
_____
_____
_____

Connecting References/Notes:

_____
_____
_____

Interpretation:

_____
_____
_____
_____

Daily Template

Day/Date: _____

Digital Time: _____

Emotion: _____

Who: _____

Where: _____

When: _____

What: _____

Location of Dream: _____

Point of Reference: _____

Title: _____

Scene # _____ Content:

_____
_____
_____
_____
_____
_____
_____
_____
_____
_____
_____
_____
_____
_____
_____
_____
_____
_____
_____
_____
_____
_____
_____
_____
_____
_____
_____
_____

Extra Room

Connecting References/Notes:

Interpretation:

Daily Template

Day/Date: _____

Digital Time: _____

Emotion: _____

Who: _____

Where: _____

When: _____

What: _____

Location of Dream: _____

Point of Reference: _____

Title: _____

Scene # _____ Content:

_____

_____

_____

_____

_____

_____

_____

_____

_____

_____

_____

_____

_____

_____

_____

_____

_____

_____

_____

_____

_____

_____

_____

_____

_____

_____

_____

_____

_____

_____

_____

Extra Room

Connecting References/Notes:

Interpretation:

Daily Template

Day/Date: _____

Digital Time: _____

Emotion: _____

Who: _____

Where: _____

When: _____

What: _____

Location of Dream: _____

Point of Reference: _____

Title: _____

Scene # _____ Content:

_____

_____

_____

_____

_____

_____

_____

_____

_____

_____

_____

_____

_____

_____

_____

_____

_____

_____

_____

_____

_____

_____

_____

_____

_____

_____

_____

_____

_____

Extra Room

Connecting References/Notes:

Interpretation:

Daily Template

Day/Date: _____

Digital Time: _____

Emotion: _____

Who: _____

Where: _____

When: _____

What: _____

Location of Dream: _____

Point of Reference: _____

Title: _____

Scene # _____ Content:

_____

_____

_____

_____

_____

_____

_____

_____

_____

_____

_____

_____

_____

_____

_____

_____

_____

_____

_____

_____

_____

_____

_____

_____

_____

_____

_____

_____

Extra Room

Connecting References/Notes:

Interpretation:

Daily Template

Day/Date: _____

Digital Time: _____

Emotion: _____

Who: _____

Where: _____

When: _____

What: _____

Location of Dream: _____

Point of Reference: _____

Title: _____

Scene # _____ Content:

_____

_____

_____

_____

_____

_____

_____

_____

_____

_____

_____

_____

_____

_____

_____

_____

_____

_____

_____

_____

_____

_____

_____

_____

_____

_____

_____

_____

_____

Extra Room

Connecting References/Notes:

Interpretation:

Daily Template

Day/Date: _____

Digital Time: _____

Emotion: _____

Who: _____

Where: _____

When: _____

What: _____

Location of Dream: _____

Point of Reference: _____

Title: _____

Scene # _____ Content:

_____

_____

_____

_____

_____

_____

_____

_____

_____

_____

_____

_____

_____

_____

_____

_____

_____

_____

_____

_____

_____

_____

_____

_____

_____

_____

_____

_____

Extra Room

Connecting References/Notes:

Interpretation:

Daily Template

Day/Date: _____

Digital Time: _____

Emotion: _____

Who: _____

Where: _____

When: _____

What: _____

Location of Dream: _____

Point of Reference: _____

Title: _____

Scene # _____ Content:

_____

_____

_____

_____

_____

_____

_____

_____

_____

_____

_____

_____

_____

_____

_____

_____

_____

_____

_____

_____

_____

_____

_____

_____

_____

_____

_____

_____

_____

_____

Extra Room

Connecting References/Notes:

Interpretation:

Daily Template

Day/Date: _____

Digital Time: _____

Emotion: _____

Who: _____

Where: _____

When: _____

What: _____

Location of Dream: _____

Point of Reference: _____

Title: _____

Scene # _____ Content:

_____
_____
_____
_____
_____
_____
_____
_____
_____
_____
_____
_____
_____
_____
_____
_____
_____
_____
_____
_____
_____
_____
_____
_____
_____
_____
_____
_____

Extra Room

Connecting References/Notes:

Interpretation:

Daily Template

Day/Date: _____

Digital Time: _____

Emotion: _____

Who: _____

Where: _____

When: _____

What: _____

Location of Dream: _____

Point of Reference: _____

Title: _____

Scene # _____ Content:

_____

_____

_____

_____

_____

_____

_____

_____

_____

_____

_____

_____

_____

_____

_____

_____

_____

_____

_____

_____

_____

_____

_____

_____

_____

_____

_____

_____

_____

Extra Room

Connecting References/Notes:

Interpretation:

Daily Template

Day/Date: _____

Digital Time: _____

Emotion: _____

Who: _____

Where: _____

When: _____

What: _____

Location of Dream: _____

Point of Reference: _____

Title: _____

Scene # _____ Content:

_____

_____

_____

_____

_____

_____

_____

_____

_____

_____

_____

_____

_____

_____

_____

_____

_____

_____

_____

_____

_____

_____

_____

_____

_____

_____

_____

_____

_____

_____

Extra Room

Connecting References/Notes:

Interpretation:

Daily Template

Day/Date: _____

Digital Time: _____

Emotion: _____

Who: _____

Where: _____

When: _____

What: _____

Location of Dream: _____

Point of Reference: _____

Title: _____

Scene # _____ Content:

_____

_____

_____

_____

_____

_____

_____

_____

_____

_____

_____

_____

_____

_____

_____

_____

_____

_____

_____

_____

_____

_____

_____

_____

_____

_____

_____

_____

_____

_____

Extra Room

Connecting References/Notes:

Interpretation:

Daily Template

Day/Date: _____

Digital Time: _____

Emotion: _____

Who: _____

Where: _____

When: _____

What: _____

Location of Dream: _____

Point of Reference: _____

Title: _____

Scene # _____ Content:

_____

_____

_____

_____

_____

_____

_____

_____

_____

_____

_____

_____

_____

_____

_____

_____

_____

_____

_____

_____

_____

_____

_____

_____

_____

_____

_____

Extra Room

Connecting References/Notes:

Interpretation:

Daily Template

Day/Date: _____

Digital Time: _____

Emotion: _____

Who: _____

Where: _____

When: _____

What: _____

Location of Dream: _____

Point of Reference: _____

Title: _____

Scene # _____ Content:

_____
_____
_____
_____
_____
_____
_____
_____
_____
_____
_____
_____
_____
_____
_____
_____
_____
_____
_____
_____
_____
_____
_____
_____
_____
_____
_____
_____

Extra Room

Connecting References/Notes:

Interpretation:

Daily Template

Day/Date: _____

Digital Time: _____

Emotion: _____

Who: _____

Where: _____

When: _____

What: _____

Location of Dream: _____

Point of Reference: _____

Title: _____

Scene # _____ Content:

_____

_____

_____

_____

_____

_____

_____

_____

_____

_____

_____

_____

_____

_____

_____

_____

_____

_____

_____

_____

_____

_____

_____

_____

_____

_____

_____

_____

_____

_____

Extra Room

Connecting References/Notes:

Interpretation:

Daily Template

Day/Date: _____

Digital Time: _____

Emotion: _____

Who: _____

Where: _____

When: _____

What: _____

Location of Dream: _____

Point of Reference: _____

Title: _____

Scene # _____ Content:

_____

_____

_____

_____

_____

_____

_____

_____

_____

_____

_____

_____

_____

_____

_____

_____

_____

_____

_____

_____

_____

_____

_____

_____

_____

_____

_____

_____

_____

_____

Extra Room

Connecting References/Notes:

Interpretation:

Daily Template

Day/Date: _____

Digital Time: _____

Emotion: _____

Who: _____

Where: _____

When: _____

What: _____

Location of Dream: _____

Point of Reference: _____

Title: _____

Scene # _____ Content:

_____

_____

_____

_____

_____

_____

_____

_____

_____

_____

_____

_____

_____

_____

_____

_____

_____

_____

_____

_____

_____

_____

_____

_____

_____

_____

_____

_____

_____

Extra Room

Connecting References/Notes:

Interpretation:

Name Interpretation Log

Family:

_____
_____
_____
_____
_____
_____
_____
_____
_____

Friends:

_____
_____
_____
_____
_____
_____
_____
_____
_____

Relationships:

_____
_____
_____
_____
_____
_____
_____
_____
_____

Symbol Library
Written in collaboration with the NIT Staff

This is not your typical Symbol Library. You won't find the most basic elements here.
Those resources are readily available other places.
These symbols are a collection from our dream work on www.nowinterpretthis.com.
You'll find that every symbol has a
"positive" and "negative" interpretation. So take your time. Browse
through and utilize what is relative to your own dreams.

ABOVE THE WAIST
Positive: Sustenance for the young, nurture
Negative: Nothing to give, without sustenance

BELOW THE WAIST
Positive: Fruit bearing
Negative: Defilement, false pregnancy

ALLEY
Positive: Something you enjoy (right up your alley)
Negative: Spiritually dark place, open to attack, place garbage/refuse is kept

ALMONDS
Positive: Resilience, healthy, begin bearing fruit after 3rd year of planting
Negative: Difficult to digest, hard-shelled

AMERICA
Positive: Freedom, prosperity
Negative: Pride, Idolatry

AMORITE
Positive: To speak
Negative: Bossy or haughty spirit

ANIMALS
Positive: Generally represent their nature (specific animal characteristics) represent dreamer's emotions (good or bad)
Negative: The unclean/immature, non-teachable, stubborn

CAT
Positive: Agile, many lives, stray (a need to belong)
Negative: Independent spirit, aloof, witchcraft

CHICKEN
Positive: Wise caution
Negative: Cowardice, jumpy, unable to stand in the face of opposition

COBRA
Positive: Armed helicopter for military warfare
Negative: Control and manipulation, far reaching evil intent, witchcraft, venomous

COW
Positive: Wealth, provision, mature meat, resource expansion
Negative: Idolatry as in "sacred cow/golden calf"

BULL
Positive: Strong, Bull Market (creating long term wealth), expeditious rise in investment value
Negative: Greed, financial entrapment, Wall Street

DOG
Positive: Companion, loyalty, best friend, guardian
Negative: Devourer, attack, characteristics of the breed
HERDING BREEDS
Positive: Herders, care takers, shepherds
Negative: Little variation in service, acknowledge only one of their talents and refuse to do anything else
GUARDING/FIGHTING BREEDS
Positive: Guardians, protective
Negative: Fierce, intimidation
MASTIFF
Positive: Guard, strong protector, powerful words
Negative: Play on words ("mass stiff" or "make stiff"), paralysis over the masses, paralyzing fear
FISH
Positive: People, souls, provision, schools of thought
Negative: Masses moving the same direction (good or bad)
HIPPO
Positive: Greek for horse, territorial in nature, protective
Negative: Dangerous person who is comfortable operating in the religious or secular world, big mouthed or bossy
HORSE
Positive: Power, authority, faith, warfare, leadership
Negative: Unleashed random/misdirected power (run-away), out of control
HUMMINGBIRD
Positive: Drawn to beauty and sweetness, partaking where it can get the most "juice", Long tongue can bypass bitter outer layers to find hidden sweetness, very effective-high levels of energy and metabolism
Negative: Flitting from one thing to another, moving too quickly to savor a moment, ineffective use of energy, non-productive
LION
Positive: Jesus, Redeemer, King, voice of protection/identity over loved ones
Negative: Satan, devourer, thief, destruction, false/wrongful proclamation over the innocent
MONKEY
Positive: Has ability similar to their maker, Bishop in some religious traditions (can denote either jurisdictional authority or ceremonial precedence)
Negative: Mocker (monkey see, monkey do), addiction (monkey on your back), childish/mischievous in nature
MOOSE/ELK
Positive: Powerful, circumpolar (distribution)
A pattern of distribution in temperate and/or arctic waters more or less surrounding either of the earth's poles. Having the ability to stand in contrasting conditions without discomfort
Negative: Unpredictable and powerful, Secret society (Loyal order of Moose)
PIG
Positive: Roots/digs for what is desired in the messiest conditions

Negative: Usually unclean, not kosher, not acceptable, messy person, someone who doesn't value what has a great price

RABBIT

Positive: Multiplication, prolific

Negative: Unclean reproduction

SKUNK

Positive: Definitive method, clear lines, decisive

Negative: Coward, but toxic when confronted

TIGER

Positive: Strong, svelte, graceful, confident, a force to be reckoned with, fortitude/speed (a tiger in your tank)

Negative: Danger, destruction, quietly stalking, wears stripes (strong contrast), guarded lines with overbearing vigilance

APARTMENTS

Positive: Community, close neighbors

Negative: Uniformity, all the same layout, limited privacy

ARM

Positive: Power, authority, the arm of the Lord

Negative: Your own strength, the strength of man, denying the power of Creator

ARROW

Positive: Direction (pointing to something), sharp/concise word, weapon

Negative: Sharp/harsh words or thoughts directed at an individual

ARTIST

Positive: Creative, right-brained/go with the flow mentality

Negative: Lacks in practicality/organizational skills, more sensitive/emotional

ASLEEP

Positive: Rest, recuperation, deep healing

Negative: Unaware, ignorance, death

AUTO PARTS

Positive: Parts of the body of Christ pertaining to ministry, characteristics of the use of the part

Negative: Parts missing/out of use (obsolete)

BABY

Positive: New thing, new project, new responsibility, something in need of your attention

Negative: Immature, elementary, missing formative stages of growth, stunted

BACK

Positive: Past (good or bad)

Negative: Vulnerability, past injuries/wounding

BACK SEAT

Positive: Along for the ride, comfortable with someone else in driver seat

Negative: Helpless in a controlled situation, past

BACK YARD

Positive: Healed past issue (dealt with), circumstances in recent past (good or bad)

Negative: Past issue not readily seen (unfinished business)

BAKING

Positive: Establishing comfort, reminder of home

Negative: Over indulgence, self-medicating with food

BALD

Positive: Cleansed of old mindsets, clean slate

Negative: State of mourning/grief

BANANA

Positive: Tender-hearted, nutritious

Negative: Slippery, dangerous under foot/to your walk

GREEN BANANA

Positive: Timing, good for intestinal health and digestion

Negative: Premature, not ready yet

BAREFOOT

Positive: Free spirited, childlike

Negative: Unprepared, no peace

BARN

Positive: Place to put harvest, storage, provision

Negative: Uncivilized, characteristics like a farm animal

BASEMENT

Positive: Deep seated structure, deeply established

Negative: Unseen/hidden, issues below the surface, storage of unnecessary items, bloodline related issue

BEARD

Positive: Filter on heart motives, protected/heartfelt speech, prudent

Negative: Cover up, hiding true motives

BED

Positive: Rest, intimacy

Negative: Inactive, slothful, apathy, hopelessness

BUILDING

Positive: Spiritually built up, corporate body/organization, a structure (good or bad)

Negative: Wicked/corrupt structure

HIGH RISE

Positive: Multiple-level system of government

Negative: Control or inheritance (good or bad), many layers, conglomerate

BIKE

Positive: Messenger (newspaper delivery), advancing from being on foot

Negative: Striving, fueled by your own strength

BLACK AND WHITE

Positive: Dramatic contrast, clear boundaries, set lines

Negative: Religious/legalistic mindset, seeing everything as black or white

BLANKET

Positive: Covering, warmth, comfort

Negative: Bondage to controlling structures, smothered

BOOK

Positive: Learning, knowledge, person/situation/organization (can't judge a book by it's cover), open (open book)

Negative: Judgment, pride in intellectualism

BOSS

Positive: Authority, Creator God, mentor

Negative: Bossy person, a stronghold of bondage

BOWLS

Positive: Vessel for worship or other interaction with heaven

Negative: Doctrine, tradition, pride

BOX

Positive: Storage, safety

Negative: Restricted, the norm, mediocre

TYPE OF BOX

Positive: Cardboard (temporary), wood (built for longevity), metal (built for security)

Negative: Limitations

BREAD

Positive: Word of God, sustenance, resources released

Negative: Withholding supply to those in need

BRIDGE

Positive: Support, joins two places, transition, overcoming obstacles

Negative: Forced transition, forcing God's hand, not waiting for God to supply the mechanism to get you over

BROTHER

Positive: Jesus, yourself, what your brother's name means, a spiritual brother

Negative: Illicit brotherhood, wrongful association/agreement

BUGS

Positive: Efficiency, diligence (ants/beetles), industrious, "bug in your ear"

Negative: Bug in system, problem, neglect

ANTS

Positive: Perseverance, application, laborious workers, industrious, diligent against greater odds, preparation, teamwork

Negative: Thieves, stinging/biting words, premeditated angry planning

BEETLES

Positive: Diligent and hard working, sometimes using ingenuity to produce an effective tool from unexpected materials

Negative: Collect feces for building purposes

MOSQUITO

Positive: Tenacious, elusive, WWII fighter/bomber (warrior)

Negative: Small annoyance that sucks the life out of you, indicator of stagnant water, transmitter of disease

ROACHES

Positive: Quick, out of sight, covert multiplication

Negative: Infestation, unclean

BURGER KING

Positive: King or authority in a particular form of teaching (healthy or unhealthy food)

Negative: Unhealthy leadership/covering, distributing false teaching to the masses for quick/easy money

BUSH

Positive: Creator God's presence, critical message

Negative: Hiding place, diversion

BUSINESS

Positive: Flourishing/successful, establishment of government, supply, inheritance (good or bad)

Negative: A mess, heavy responsibility
CABINETS
Positive: Storage for service elements, needed equipment
Negative: Hiding elements out of use/obsolete
UPPER CABINETS
Positive: Higher thoughts
Negative: Limited access
LOWER CABINETS
Positive: Easy access
Negative: Lower mentality, hopeless mindsets
CAMP
Positive: Temporary residence, rest, passing through/stopping over place
Negative: To "camp out" rather than moving on, transitional situation (good or bad)
CANAANITE
Positive: Humble or subdued
Negative: Lust, addiction
CANDLES
Positive: Enlightenment, celebration, intercession
Negative: Limited revelation, dim or under established
CAR
Positive: You, personal ministry, characteristics of vehicle, job, spiritual journey
Negative: Lazy, not willing to build strength/stamina, desire to arrive quickly
CARPOOLER
Positive: Someone going the same direction as you,
someone in ministry with you, what your carpooler's name means
Negative: Opposing force/relationship drawing you off course
CELESTIAL
Positive: Pertaining to sky or Heaven, spirit beings
Negative: Familiar spirits that live/travel 2nd heaven (earth's atmosphere)
CEREAL
Positive: Starter food for the spiritually immature
Negative: Lacking in nourishment to further growth
CHILDREN
Positive: God's children, the spiritually immature/young
Negative: Undernourished, malnourished
YOUR CHILDREN
Positive: Yourself, themselves or the meaning of their names, babies at something
Negative: Rebellious children, pride
CHURCH
Positive: Congregation, gathering of individuals for/in worship
Negative: Age-old traditions, false religion
OLD CHURCH
Positive: Inheritance, great heritage
Negative: Old traditions, belief, set system, ritualistic religion
CLIFF
Positive: On the edge, risk, change
Negative: Danger, over the edge

CLIMBING

Positive: Advancement, paying the price for a great reward

Negative: Difficulty, opposition

CLOSET

Positive: Prayer/intercession, private chamber, hidden away

Negative: Hiding out, storing up, isolation

CLOTHING/ATTIRE

Positive: Covering of mindsets, attitudes, emotions, denotes status/authority/commissioning, changes with activity

Negative: Costume, habit, dressing up to deceive/pretend

DRESS

Positive: Femininity, covering, anointing, call or occupation

Negative: Inappropriate, impractical or indecent for physical or manual labor

PANTS

Positive: Authority, work, consider style, what you're walking in

Negative: Bossy (wearing the pants), illegal authority, keeping the upper hand

SHIRT

Positive: Covering of the heart

Negative: Defense to cover or guard the heart, walls

SKIRT

Positive: Covering, grace

Negative: Avoiding a situation

COBWEB

Positive: Intricate networking not yet in use

Negative: Neglect, dormant, webbing that holds you in

COFFEE

Positive: A wake up call, jump-start on your day, pungent fragrance, comfort

Negative: Acidity, bitterness, diuretic causing dehydration

COLLEGE

Positive: Place of training, "higher" education

Negative: Party atmosphere, not taking things seriously

COMMISSION

Positive: Military/strategic orders or approval for a specific assignment

Negative: Variant structure of pay, not always a set paycheck

CONGESTION

Positive: Grace for stinky situations, you take things in stride

Negative: Unable to take in what is needed, plugged up, "traffic jam"

CONVERTIBLE

Positive: Open Heaven, freedom (wind in your hair)

Negative: Open to the elements, uncovered

COOLER

Positive: Preserves food (word), chiller as in "chilling"

Negative: Diffuses passion, procrastination, indecision

COPS

Positive: Authority (good or bad), covert spiritual enforcers working for the Kingdom of God

Negative: Enforcers of the curse of the law

COUSIN
Positive: Something related, distant family
Negative: Family jealousy/tension, family competition

CRYING
Positive: Cleansing, release
Negative: Grief, anguish, mourning

DARK
Positive: Hidden, covert, under cover assignment, dark but lovely (Creator's unconditional love for humanity)
Negative: Ignorance, power of evil, blind

DEATH
Positive: Death to self, new found trust in Creator God
Negative: Termination, something coming to an end (good or bad), ignorance

DECORATOR
Positive: Creator, designer, the great architect
Negative: False or illegal administration/management

DIARRHEA
Positive: Exponential deliverance/release of contaminants
Negative: "Running off at the mouth," uncontrollable contamination or defilement

DINING ROOM
Positive: Place of fellowship, serving people, eating spiritual food
Negative: Breaking bread in broken fellowship

DIRT ROAD
Positive: Future direction, not yet constructed
Negative: Unclean, going your way rather than the best way, premature

DOCTOR
Positive: Jesus, Healer, trusted individual offering help
Negative: Treatment from outside/not trusted source

DOOR
Positive: Entry, endeavor, opportunity, security, protection
Negative: Forced entry, unlocked, left open for thieves or worse

DRUG STORE
Positive: Helpful medication for healing
Negative: Spiritual senses numbed (drugged up)

DRUNK
Positive: Drunk in the Spirit, under the influence
Negative: Impaired judgment, counterfeit of being Spirit- filled

DUMP
Positive: To rid oneself of unnecessary objects/issues
Negative: Corruption, used up

EARRINGS
Positive: Calls attention to hearing, prophetic hearing, clarity
Negative: Diversion from clear hearing

EUCALYPTAS
Positive: A healing authority or leadership, part of the Myrtle tree family
Negative: Excessive or strong personality

EX-BOYFRIEND/HUSBAND
Positive: First love (Jesus), that which you've successfully cut ties with, past experiences/associations
Negative: Bondage to old lifestyles/situations, unhealthy associations
EYES
Positive: Windows of the soul, desire, revelation, understanding
Negative: Give away, the tell, cannot lie
FACE
Positive: Reveals the heart, emotions, expression
Negative: False impressions, putting on appearances, mask
FACTORY
Positive: Production, diverse specific tasks of service, manufacturing
Negative: Lack of individuality, uniformity, assembly line
FAMILY
Positive: Actual family, spiritual family
Negative: Bloodline issues, adverse hereditary patterns
FAN
Positive: Focused wind of God's Spirit
Negative: Human induced coercion
FEET
Positive: Works, pertaining to your walk, slow/steady progress, your stand, preparation
Negative: Operating in your own strength, bare feet (lack of preparation)
FENCE
Positive: Boundary, protection, security
Negative: Containment, held or "fenced in," religious tradition
FIELD
Positive: The world, place of harvest, profession, day of enjoyment (field day) "playing field", opportunity for cultivation, sphere of influence
Negative: Racket, weakness, misuse of connections
FINGER
Positive: Discerning, conviction, one of the 5-fold ministries
Negative: Pointing, judgment
THUMB
Positive: Apostle, authority, builder, equipper, visionary
Negative: Under thumb or control
INDEX FINGER
Positive: Prophet, messages of encouragement, edification, comfort
Negative: False words/motives, pointing, judgment
MIDDLE FINGER
Positive: Evangelist, one who carries influence to draw many to his/her cause
Negative: Wicked influence over the masses
RING FINGER
Positive: Pastor, lover of covenant and is the shepherd
Negative: May lead astray with false teaching
PINKY FINGER
Positive: Teacher, impartation, mentor

Negative: Teacher of false doctrine, lies

FLOOR
Positive: Foundational, beliefs that we stand upon
Negative: Lowest plane of a space, deep-seated traditions

CEMENT FLOOR
Positive: Gospel, established
Negative: Hard and cold

FLOUR
Positive: Sacrifice, offering, the base for bread, home made
Negative: Thickens, hardens into solid object, restricts movement

FOG
Positive: Under cover, covert, hidden
Negative: Cannot see situation clearly, thick covering

FOOD
Positive: Word of God, foundational, truth, manna
Negative: Damaging words, false message, spoiled manna (wrong timing)

FOOTBALL
Positive: Warfare, social involvement
Negative: Competition, idolatry

FOREIGNER
Positive: From a different place/mindset/culture/language, outsider
Negative: Alien, malicious

FOREST
Positive: Group of leaders, covering, safety
Negative: Adversity, blinders, lack of vision for your surroundings

FOUR-WHEELER/4 WHEEL DRIVE
Positive: Ministry that goes places others can't, (All Terrain Vehicle), Utilitarian, 4 x 4 = ruling over land/territory, sudden change
Negative: Not the smoothest ride, can have a greater price

FRIENDS
Positive: Represent the dreamer, the characteristic of that friend, the friend in your dream (good or bad)
Negative: Adverse influence, negative popular opinion

FRONT
Positive: Present or future revealed
Negative: Exposed, something used as a masking device

FRONT END LOADER
Positive: Earth moving ministry, used to clear ground, transports construction materials, something moved for future work
Negative: Destructive, demolition, leveling

FRONT YARD
Positive: Present or future, what's plain to see (it's right out there)
Negative: Exposed, revealed to passers-by/pirates/thieves

FURNITURE
Positive: Attitudes, mindsets, things you keep around you, type of furniture is important, the traditions you seat yourself upon
Negative: Furnishing your life with untruth, false doctrine, damaging/adverse tradition

GANGSTER
Positive: Member of a family, protection for family members from outside sources
Negative: Spirit of fear or intimidation, fatherless

GARAGE
Positive: Rest from ministry, storage and overflow
Negative: Stagnant, procrastination

GETHSEMANE
Positive: Oil or olive press, benefits of dying to self, complete obedience
Negative: Trials, difficult decision, in the process

GIFT
Positive: Unearned reward, free from reciprocation
Negative: Strings attached, manipulation

GLASS
Positive: Transparency, clarity, eyes to see
Negative: Unseen restriction, deceptive barrier

CRACKED GLASS
Positive: Breaking out
Negative: Peace disturbed, accusations

GLUE
Positive: Adheres, sticks to, needed bonding
Negative: Bondage, captivity

GODMOTHER
Positive: Spiritual mother (good or bad), structure or organization/association you are a part of (good or bad)
Negative: Idolatry, strong influence

GRASS
Positive: New growth, flourishing, fertile territory, earth's covering
Negative: Flesh, needs regular maintenance, mixture with weeds

GREEN ACRES
Positive: A happy place, happier/simpler days, flourishing times
Negative: Not happy with present circumstances, desiring greener pastures

GROUP
Positive: Merging aspects of one's character, a body or system
Negative: Mass influence, peer pressure

HAIR
Positive: Covering, mindsets, paradigms
Negative: Overgrowth due to neglect, not maintaining

HAIRCUT
Positive: Releasing old mindsets, getting a "new look"
Negative: Losing the results of slow/steady growth, changing original identity

HALLWAY
Positive: Transition, birth canal
Negative: Narrow place, darkness, tight spot, constricting

HANDS
Positive: Service, relationship, work, agreement, connection
Negative: Works in the flesh, inflicting injury in wrongful outreach/motives

LEFT HAND
Positive: Holds weapon, dependence upon a greater force

Negative: Hesitation/weakness in physical action or response

RIGHT HAND

Positive: Holds ammunition, Creator's justice released

Negative: Judgment, operating in one's own strength

HAT

Positive: Covering, thoughts, attitudes, consider type of hat

Negative: Limiting oneself to only one occupational activity

BASEBALL CAP

Positive: In the game, informal

Negative: Inappropriate attire for some functions

CONSTRUCTION HAT

Positive: Protection, occupation

Negative: Hardheaded, shielded mindsets, stubborn beliefs

HEAD

Positive: Authority, reigning officer, protector

Negative: False authority, leadership with wrongful motives, manipulation

HEADPHONES

Positive: Message for your ears only, hearing in stereo

Negative: Hearing impairment, undermining, subversion

HEART ATTACK

Positive: Painful truth which brings healing

Negative: Emotional pain which affects other parts of the body

HIGHWAY

Positive: Right way, fast way, your life or way of living

Negative: Potential danger if moving too slowly or in the wrong lane

HILL

Positive: Spiritual advancement, integrity, in right standing

Negative: Uphill battle, opposition

HONEY

Positive: Strength, wisdom, word, anointing, nectar of the righteous, intense nourishment, truth spoken in love

Negative: Flattery, sticky, trap

HORN

Positive: Ruler, authority, power, head of kingdom, kingdom with military force

Negative: Wicked authority, corruption, false leadership

HOSPITAL

Positive: Place of healing, place to gain "patience" or to be tested, assessment of bloodline or spiritual make up

Negative: Opening for occult spirits, established strongholds, infirmed

HOTEL

Positive: Temporary place, transition, public place of business, hospitality

Negative: Lack of privacy, noisy, dealing with the issues of those around you

HOUSE

Positive: Your life, your current condition (good or bad), meaning of family name

Negative: Established strongholds/bondage

PARENT'S HOUSE

Positive: Generational inheritance, security, home

Negative: Generational strongholds, familiarity
HUNGER
Positive: Spiritual hunger, yearning for more of the good
Negative: Void, without nourishment
HUNTING
Positive: Searching, going after the "meat" of the word, diligent in seeking
Negative: Predator, prey
HUSBAND
Positive: Jesus, authority, something/someone you are associated with (good or bad)
Negative: Control, abusive authority, in agreement with a counteractive/detrimental source
ICICLE
Positive: Sharp, useful weaponry, piercing/melting the heart
Negative: Hard heart, cold or frigid attitude
INTERNATIONAL HARVESTER
Positive: One who will glean from or influence the nations
Negative: Devourer, thief of needed resources on a global basis
INTERSTATE
Positive: Existing or carried between states/condition
Negative: Spreading of contaminants from one territory/state/condition to another
ISLAND
Positive: Completely dependent upon Creator God, is not influenced by others, flint-faced
Negative: Isolation, separation, independent of others, self-reliant
JEANS
Positive: What you're walking in (good or bad), versatility, everyday wear, possible reference to Levites
Negative: Inappropriate for many environments, rebellious
JEBUSITE
Positive: To trample down in war, descendents of the faithful Noah
Negative: Religious spirit, treading down, destructive, seduction
JUNGLE GYM
Positive: Recreational climbing, strengthens muscles and builds greater stamina, varied body building activities
Negative: Childish activities, operating in the past
KENNEL
Positive: Safety, security, safely supervised place to run
Negative: Constrained, limited, caged talents
KEYS
Positive: Authority, understanding, revelation, access to new areas, way out, needed tools of efficiency
Negative: Locks portals of opportunity, holds resources out/in
KEYSTONE
Positive: The stability of an entrance, portal or opportunity, holds the weight of the opening/stabilizes
Negative: Secures/sets limitations in openings/opportunities

KITCHEN
Positive: Heart of something, intent, motive, ambition, place where spiritual food is prepared
Negative: Over-indulgence, obesity, inactive in using gifts
KNEES
Positive: Humility, prayer/intercession, service
Negative: Blockage, lack of hearing, obstinate
LADY
Positive: Spirit (good or evil), Holy Spirit, meaning of her name, beauty/grace, womanhood
Negative: Controlling, alluring, entrapment, lust
LAGOON
Positive: Holding place for treatment of contamination, safe haven for messengers/itinerant workers to rest
Negative: Stagnant, isolated, shallow, mixture, not useful, restricted flow of the Spirit
LAKE
Positive: Place of peace/relaxation, clear view, reservoir of resources
Negative: No movement, limited resources
LAMP
Positive: Illumination, clear path, exposing what's in the darkness
Negative: Casting shadows, limited revelation, without fuel/power
LAND
Positive: Sphere of influence, territory, nation, to arrive at a destination
Negative: Illegal influence, outside of one's authority, wrongful squatting
LATE
Positive: Prudence, wisdom, caution
Negative: Out of proper timing, unprepared, often caused by resistance, overdue
LATTICE
Positive: Privacy, flourishing, weaving to build a structure
Negative: Obscuring, blocking, misrepresentation
LAUNDRY
Positive: Clean (cleaning) clothes or attitudes
Negative: Unclean, filth, used/soiled
LAUNDRY ROOM
Positive: Place of cleansing, changing attitudes/emotions
Negative: Collection of that which is unclean
LEFT
Positive: Strength of God/Creator, arm of the Lord
Negative: Weakness of man
LEFT TURN
Positive: Spiritual change, adjustment
Negative: Independent of Creator
LEG
Positive: Walk, strength, power, pillar, defense, mainstay
Negative: Rebellious (kicking and screaming), stubborn, weak, taking the wrong path
LEMON
Positive: Opportunity to overcome, fresh, antioxidant (cleansing), natural softener

Negative: Sour, bad deal, duped, deceived, attacks wisdom

LIGHT

Positive: Security, wellbeing, knowledge, revelation, truth

Negative: Exposing imperfections harshly, casting shadows

LINEN

Positive: Purity, all natural, intrinsic beauty

Negative: Imperfection, easily wrinkles

LIVING ROOM

Positive: Revealed, everyday or current affairs, truth exposed without hypocrisy, social, entertainment

Negative: Life exposed to selective few, bringing things or people in close without wisdom or prudence

LOCKER

Positive: Safe storage, accessible during times of transition or activity, supplies for next period in life, cooler for food

Negative: Not accessible, locked up, hyper-vigilance

LOT

Positive: Property, responsibility; circumstances in life (good or bad), allotted portion by inheritance, one's fate or destiny (good or bad)

Negative: Choice by chance in making bets (settling for what may come), to "lot out" or mark for deletion, to mark as obsolete

LUMBER

Positive: Building material, most commonly used element for framing construction in residential building

Negative: Wood-flesh, easily catches fire and burns quickly, volatile in certain climate and harsh weather conditions

LUNCH

Positive: Spiritual enrichment, enlightenment

Negative: Break in a productive day, can be diversion from efficiency, stretching your lunch break out

MAGNET

Positive: Evangelistic, attracts, draws to oneself

Negative: Controlling force/coercion

MAKE-UP

Positive: What you are made of, your resolution/fortitude

Negative: Mask, cover-up, appearances, hiding flaws

MALL

Positive: Marketplace with variety, choices of garments/attitudes, "need for change," public governmental platform as in Washington DC

Negative: Distraction, too many choices, indecision

MANAGER

Positive: Authority figure (good or bad), coach/mentor, one who trains in protocol for the better of all, protection, security

Negative: One who controls, limitations, undermining of your talent/ability

MAP

Positive: Direction, correction, advice, Word of God/Creator

Negative: Diversion, misleading, false direction

MEAT
Positive: Solid food, Word of God/Creator, nutrients
Negative: Too much to digest, too heavy for the immature

MIDNIGHT
Positive: (The Western Calendar) the hour an old structure ends, the beginning of a new day, order of government for new day
Negative: Hour of hidden/occult activity

MIRROR
Positive: Reflection, consideration, imagination, impression
Negative: Copy, deception (smoke and mirrors)

MOBILE PHONE
Positive: Constant communication, convenience, security
Negative: Distraction, disturbance, diversion, communication from outside sources

MONRDRIAN ART
Positive: Apparent simplicity with infinite varied, subtle and complex elements, staggered symmetry, out of the box
Negative: Can cause negative reaction in an atmosphere where only familiar lines and movement are accepted

MONEY
Positive: Resources, provision, currency, power, security
Negative: The love of which brings corruption/destruction

MOTHER-IN-LAW
Positive: Added support structure, what her name means
Negative: Meddler, legalistic church or spiritual influence

MOTOR HOME
Positive: Temporary living quarters, versatility and the ability to live in many places, mobility, itinerant ministry
Negative: Wandering, inability to put down roots,

MOUNTAIN
Positive: Establishment of God the Creator, kingdom (good or bad), advancement
Negative: Obstacle, high place utilized by outside sources

MULBERRY TREE
Positive: Announces a victory already won on your behalf
Negative: Failure to identify/acknowledge your victory, not giving credit where credit is due

MUSIC
Positive: Worship, release of joy and freedom, the sound of one's DNA, a message from creator
Negative: False sound, distorted as in a copy of a copy

MUSTACHE
Positive: Filtered speech (speech sweep), prudent in efforts
Negative: Masked threat

NAILS
Positive: Words, fully secured, efficient/sturdy construction
Negative: Hard cold truth delivered in a harsh manner, painful life construction, hard truth

NAKED
Positive: Vulnerable, open, transparent

Negative: Without covering, exposed

NAMES

Positive: Generally meaning of the name, person's label or identity

Negative: Words spoken out of ignorance, false labels

NEIGHBOR

Positive: Friendship, loyalty (true or false)

Negative: Too close for comfort, seeing what your life is really like

NEWSPAPER

Positive: Prophetic revelation, current events, headliner

Negative: Published information, not necessarily accurate or truth, propaganda

NIGHT

Positive: Hidden, under cover, covert, sight into supernatural realm

Negative: Evil, ignorance, deception

NUTS AND BOLTS

Positive: The essentials, holds it all together

Negative: Inanimate/ineffective make-up or false design, too practical, cut and dry

OUTSIDE

Positive: Interacting with the world, out of the ordinary (outside the box)

Negative: Not fitting in, isolated, exposed, not in fellowship

PARKING GARAGE

Positive: Slow down, stop, a season of rest and restoration

Negative: Holding or idle place for personal ministry or life, congregation of the idle

PASTOR

Positive: Spiritual Leader (good or bad), mentor, shepherd

Negative: False authority, false or unrighteous mentoring, control, spiritual abuse

PATH

Positive: Your direction in life, personal walk

Negative: False inheritance established by the wicked in your bloodline

PEN/PENCIL

Positive: Pertains to the written word, the tongue, the creative word, vision

Negative: Indelible, words that take, words used in witchcraft

PET

Positive: Something you are feeding (good or bad), something precious

Negative: Pet issue, something you continue to feed or rehearse

PHARMACY

Positive: Medicinal, chemistry, receiving prescription

Negative: Place to receive drugs/narcotics, self-medicating, medicating symptoms instead of the cause

PHONE

Positive: Communication, prayer, clear connection from Creator

Negative: Bad or static connection/dropping calls from an outside source

PICTURE FRAME

Positive: Focused attention to vision or memory, territory/landscape with boundaries (good or bad), beginning of new construction, spiritual physique

Negative: Caging, trapped in a moment of time, a memory

PICTURE/PHOTO

Positive: Visual revelation, memory (good or bad)

Negative: Situation/emotions caught in time

PIER

Positive: Better access to deep resources, birthing outside your comfort zone, outreach

Negative: Staying on land, failure to launch

PIPE

Positive: Vessel of the Spirit, conduit, main line

Negative: Tight place, conveyer of sewage

PIT

Positive: Undesirable situation that unexpectedly leads to a blessing, a turn for the good

Negative: Trap, despair, difficult to get free from

POLICE

Positive: Authority (good or bad), enforcers of the law

Negative: Enforcers of corrupt laws, control, entrapment

POOL

Positive: Spiritual community, refreshment, condition of freedom where one can operate in their gifting

Negative: Collection of stagnation, allowed operation with limitation

PORCH

Positive: Welcome, world's view, exposed or revealed to the public, see also front or back

Negative: Opportunity of entrance for enemy, settling for sitting still

PREGNANT

Positive: Something needing to be birthed, new call, vision, endeavor or business

Negative: Prolonged or delayed delivery, fail to birth or birthing out of time

PRESCRIPTION

Positive: Written solution, decree, direction, remedy, regulation, preparation, ordinance

Negative: Law, rule, mixture, solution with negative side affects

PROPERTY

Positive: Responsibility, sphere of geographic or spiritual authority, ownership, capital

Negative: Under the control of others, tied to something with no worth

PURSE

Positive: Personal identity, supply, resources, necessities

Negative: That which is relegated to you by bloodline or name (good or bad), lack

RACE

Positive: Contest, urgent need, mandate

Negative: Competitive, limited output, relegated to a common path

RAFTERS

Positive: Supports the covering, people going with the flow, carried by a strong current

Negative: Support exposed, influenced by the crowd or popular current

RANGE ROVER

Positive: "Off road" ministry, one that can take rough terrain, off the beaten path, very specific/extraordinary calling

Negative: Wanderer, without purpose

REFRIDGERATOR

Positive: Fresh food (The encouraging word), storage, heart, preservation

Negative: Cold storage, preservation, hoarding of that which will spoil

RESTAURANT

Positive: Place for choices in spiritual food, fellowship, nourishment offered to the masses (good or bad)

Negative: Being catered to, immaturity, opting for what is easy

RIGHT

Positive: Strength of man, physical ability, grace for mankind

Negative: Judgment

RIGHT TURN

Positive: Natural change, going the "right" direction

Negative: Working in a natural mindset

RING

Positive: Covenant, promise, agreement, something you are in association with

Negative: Bound to, bondage, wrongful agreement, agreement by coercion

RIVER

Positive: Life, Spirit, free flow, resources

Negative: Strong current, flooding banks, overwhelming

ROAD

Positive: Your way of life

Negative: Wrong direction taken

ROOF

Positive: Mind, intellect, covering from the elements

Negative: Exposed, your ceiling or limitations, need for freer thinking

ROOMMATE

Positive: Brotherhood or relationship, sharing your personal space

Negative: Bunking up with the undesirable, allowing your enemy to move in

ROOTS

Positive: Origin, heart of the matter

Negative: Stubborn generational patterns

SCHOOL

Positive: Place of training, High School/college - "higher" education

Negative: Missed some important lessons, having to return to make up the time, redo

SCHOOL BUS

Positive: Learning – passenger, Teaching – driver, educational ministry or occupation

Negative: Class clown, frivolous in receiving needed knowledge, not taking serious the weight of imparting to others

SCIENTIST

Positive: Understanding of - the supernatural, God and His vast creation

Negative: Can value natural means of knowledge over the supernatural, worldly wisdom

SECRETARY

Positive: Administration, in charge of correspondence, filing, scheduling and routine duties

Negative: Overly administrative, can be compulsive obsessive, controlling

SHACK/SHANTY

Positive: Spiritually rich, humility, the belief that your riches are laid up in heaven and not here on earth

Negative: Spiritual poverty, austerity, false pride, self-denial to gain acceptance
SHOES
Positive: Your life's message, preparation, what you're walking in, consider the type
Negative: Limited preparation, preparation that is not you, preparation that is the wrong fit, type or is inappropriate in timing
NEW SHOES
Positive: New ministry, occupation, activity
Negative: New at something, still inexperienced
SILVER
Positive: Refining, knowledge, redemption, of foremost value (will not lose it's value)
Negative: Legalism, falsely refined
SINGING
Positive: Worship, flowing in your true identity, releasing undeniable joy
Negative: Snitch, tattle-tale, manipulative speech to gain acceptance
SINK
Positive: Cleansing
Negative: Going under, circling the drain
SKINLESS
Positive: Completely transparent, exhibiting your spirit instead of your flesh
Negative: Difficulty sensing external world or your own emotions, open or raw, not comfortable in your identity, not "held together," falling apart
SLIDING DOOR
Positive: Realignment, easy opening
Negative: Off-track, deceptive in appearance
SMOKE
Positive: Burning of incense in the inner court of The God of the Universe/The Living God, Glory
Negative: Deceptive covering (smoke and mirrors), fire, danger
SNOW
Positive: Purity, clean, covering, refreshing, peace
Negative: Sometimes accompanied by harsh elements, can have frigid conditions that cause injury
SPEEDBOAT
Positive: Fast progress, quick advancement above the depths
Negative: Missing some things along the way, bypassing selective parts of a beneficial process
STAIRS
Positive: Ascending or descending to a greater level of maturity, glory, education
Negative: Descending to destruction or stagnation
STARBUCKS
Positive: Community, wake up, ministry, connecting
Negative: Spirit of Siren/mermaid, lures unknowing travelers to a death structure, foolish use of money if glutinous or imprudent
STARS
Positive: People, believers, ministers, role model, also can be connected to five-fold ministry
Negative: Superstition, being enthroned on a cultural mountain or high place

STONES
Positive: Witness or testimony, an alter upon which something is built, White stone – new name given by Creator for new season/level of authority
Negative: Harmful words or judgments

SUITCASE
Positive: Transition, travel, temporary circumstances
Negative: Emotional baggage, being weighed down by extra baggage

SUV/SPORTS UTILITY VEHICLE
Positive: Good for transporting larger items and many passengers, 4-wheel drive (not deterred by severe conditions), good on rough terrain, utilitarian
Negative: Often comes with a higher price tag, propensity to carry that which is unnecessary

SWAMP
Positive: Free to move out of old unproductive situations, refuge/haven for the near extinct
Negative: Bogged down, danger of paralysis, condition of helpless inactivity

T-SHIRT
Positive: Often features graphics that project/display the person's tastes, identity, individuality and attitudes, casual, comfortable dress
Negative: Unprofessional, rebellious, tacky, under dressed or inappropriate attire for specific functions

TABLE
Positive: Fellowship, communion, agreement, what you "bring to the table" (ideas and talents)
Negative: False agreement and fellowship/relationship

TAILOR
Positive: One who cuts and sews, creator, the one who fashioned you, does alteration when needed
Negative: Forcing unnecessary/unsolicited change, construction or conformity

TAP DANCE
Positive: Keeping up with life, rapid movement, rhythm, exuberant
Negative: Dancing to please (doing the dance)

TARGET
Positive: Hitting the mark
Negative: Object of adversity, persecution

TARGET STORE (IN USA)
Positive: Better quality at a good value, better design priced for the masses
Negative: Less versatile in specific areas

TARP
Positive: Covering/protection against the elements
Negative: Unnecessary guarding, overly cautious

THIEF
Positive: Being covert to recover what was taken from you
Negative: Deception, famine, loss

TOILE WALLPAPER
Positive: Repeated story, valued or repeated history, the historical "writing on the wall," often pastoral prints depicting simpler and more romantic eras/times

Negative: Repetition, monochromatic/lack of diversity and color, set in your ways, inflexible

TOILET
Positive: Deliverance release defecation/defilement
Negative: In the toilet/circling the drain, headed for destruction

TONGUE
Positive: Creative power and spiritual ability, spiritual language, ability to articulate, confession, spiritual building tool, encouragement, prophetic edification
Negative: Ability to cut or wound, gossip, slander

TOYS
Positive: Child-like outlook, appreciation and acceptance of those who are still young in their beliefs
Negative: Child's play, false preparation, still a place of immaturity, an imitation of something effective

TRACTOR
Positive: Harvesting ministry/work, one who plows/pioneer, sowing into a ground or territory, ability to pull people out of miry circumstances
Negative: Too slow, only made to be utilitarian, not built for distance

TRAILER
Positive: Carries resources, distribution
Negative: Can be unstable on road, past issues that limit you in your present state (pull along behind you), bad baggage

TRAIN
Positive: Training, fast track, carrier of passengers
Negative: Train wreck, being railroaded, limited by one direction only

TRASH
Positive: What is no longer needed, no issue, already disposed of
Negative: Of no value, need to dispose of, corruption

TREE
Positive: Covering, leadership, family tree
Negative: Negative influence of human authority, not allowing direct access to God the Father/Creator

CROOKED TREE
Positive: Not the norm, not on the regular path, the experience of many trials
Negative: Unrighteous or deceptive authority/leadership, triggers which are caused by past mental, spiritual or emotional injury/abuse, harmful tentacles established in mind and emotions/negative roots

TRUCK (Consider the type of truck and it's use)
Positive: If new-used for new activity, form of occupation (good or bad), work
Negative: If old-out of date, not of good use

PICK UP
Positive: For "picking up," work or hauling / carrying
Negative: No room for passengers, an attempt to influence or coerce

SEMI/18-WHEELER
Positive: Carrier of resources for the masses, ample room for transport
Negative: Too large for narrow thorough-fares or city driving, dangerous (jack knife) on slick roads

CONCRETE MIXER TRUCK
Positive: Mixer for laying foundations, the beginning of construction process
Negative: Used for setting or anchoring, settling into a detrimental situation

TRUMPET
Positive: Warning, sounding alarm, creative words that break things open in the spiritual/natural world, decrees, voice of God, voice of the prophetic, gathering of the elect, announcement, jubilee, rejoicing
Negative: Call for judgment, memorial dedication usually at death (Taps), an exit

TURNING
Positive: Repentance, change, decision
Negative: Coming off the straight path, settling

RIGHT TURN
Positive: "Correct" turn, natural change (good or bad)
Negative: Change based on your own strength/the flesh

LEFT TURN
Positive: Spiritual change (good or bad), change based on dependence upon a greater force
Negative: Feeling "left out," weakness, incapability

TV
Positive: Influence (good or bad), educational, vision (tell-a-vision) revelation
Negative: Subliminal brain washing, distraction, wasting time

WALK
Positive: Progress, exercise, your life/direction
Negative: Operating in flesh / your own power, slower progress

WALL
Positive: Security, privacy
Negative: Barrier, control issue, blocked, limitation

WALMART STORE (IN USA)
Positive: Convenience, quantity over quality, good value, one stop shopping, versatility
Negative: Commonality, conformity to the masses, settling for lesser quality based upon price

WAREHOUSE
Positive: Place of provision or storage, promises, healings, gifts
Negative: Survivalist mentality, hoarding, false security

WATCH
Positive: Attention to time, relating to a window/opportunity of time, representation of the time displayed
Negative: Lack of timing, out of time, the need to be watchful

WATER
Positive: Spirit, refreshing, cleansing, critical to life, fluidity, feeling weightless
Negative: Without anchor, lack of stability, floating without direction, no connection to land

WATERFALL
Positive: Pouring out of God's Spirit, refreshing
Negative: Feeling of being overwhelmed, constant berating or rebuke

WEB
Positive: Beautifully woven or orchestrated, network

Negative: Intricate pattern of circumstances, entrapment

WHEEL

Positive: Pertaining to a cycle (good or bad), forward motion, power of synergy (wheel within a wheel)

Negative: Repetitive patterns, generational curses, addictions caused by inheritable propensities

WIFE

Positive: Someone you are in covenant with (good or bad), what her name means (good or bad), a body of people in common belief

Negative: Nag, control, wrong covenant, limitation, entrapment

WINDOW

Positive: Portal, time-sensitive opportunity, prophetic revelation, vision, insight

Negative: Opening for an enemy, adversity, vulnerability

WINTER

Positive: Opportunity for cozy comfort inside with family and friends, brisk fun in the beauty of snow fall and holidays, enjoyment of a Winter Wonderland

Negative: Little light, hardship, spiritually cold, season of no growth, dormancy

WORKMAN

Positive: Makes repairs, adjustments

Negative: Working (in the flesh) for acceptance / to validate identity

WOUND

Positive: Something opened up for purposes of healing, injury uncovered/revealed

Negative: Hurt/injury, soul or spirit damage, emotional trigger

WRIST

Positive: Relationship (good or bad)

Negative: bondage

Numbers

(1)

Positive: Alpha, God, unity, beginning

Negative: Alone, independence, isolation

(2)

Positive: Agreement, you and Creator

Negative: Division

(3)

Positive: Trinity, resurrection, established confirmation, (past, present, future)

Negative: Spirit of Antichrist, unbelief

(4)

Positive: Rule and reign, four corners of the earth, four seasons, four winds, four horsemen, wind/earth/fire/water - elements of the earth, Delta-sudden change

Negative: Alarm, warning

(5)

Positive: Grace, five positions of ministry in Evangelical Christianity, redemption, 1)Apostle, 2)Prophet, 3)Evangelist, 4)Preacher, 5)Teacher

Negative: Conditional acceptance, earned reward

(6)

Positive: Number of man, God's most beloved creation

Negative: Operating in the flesh instead of the Spirit

(7)

Positive: Perfection, completion, rest

Negative: Incomplete, waiting to be established

(8)

Positive: New beginnings, new reign or government

Negative: Illegal/corrupt governmental authority, stuck in an old season

(9)

Positive: Holy Spirit (9 gifts, 9 fruits), harvest, finale

Negative: Judgment, termination, deadline

(10)

Positive: Order, fullness, double grace

Negative: Law

(11)

Positive: Transition, gate, portal, double portion, the prophetic

Negative: Narrow place, caught "in-between"

(12)

Positive: Leadership, government, authority

Negative: Unequipped/un-ordained leadership, not appointed, illegal authority

(13)

Positive: HaShem (Judaism meaning The Name) God

Negative: Rebellion

(15)

Positive: Multiple of grace, new direction, rest

Negative: Slave's wage

(16)

Positive: New established government, fullness for man

Negative: Influence of man

(17)

Positive: Victory, fullness of completion

Negative: Waiting on established completion

(18)

Positive: Overcoming

Negative: Judgment, destruction, bondage put upon

(22)

Positive: Double gates, exponential progress, favor

Negative: Delay

(30)

Positive: Maturity for ministry, fullness of preparation

Negative: Falling behind in preparation, not ready

(50)

Positive: Freedom, jubilee, exponential grace

Negative: Extended season of bondage

(111)

Positive: Birth of Jesus, establishment of Jesus' reign

Negative: Denial that Jesus is the Son of God

(222)

Positive: Multiple of = 6 (Man), Creator's favorite creation

Negative: Divided/separated from Creator/God

(528)

Positive: (Hebrew) Love, (Hertz) Repair/building of DNA, Father's perfect love

Negative: False identity, fatherless

(800)

Positive: Omega (The end)

Negative: Denial that Creator/God is infinite

(888)

Positive: Jesus, God the beginning and the end

Negative: Void of redemption/salvation

(1000)

Positive: Maturity, fullness, Millennium

Negative: Not yet the fullness of time

Colors

BLACK
Positive: Passion, formal, sophistication, mystery
Negative: Ignorance, famine, void, evil

BLUE
Positive: Revelation, prophetic, pertaining to the heavenly realm, peace, coolness, refreshing
Negative: Aloof, depression

BROWN
Positive: Humility, pure of heart, nature
Negative: Death, drought, barrenness

CRIMSON
Positive: The Blood of Jesus, forgiveness, wine
Negative: Blood, death

GOLD
Positive: Glory, holy, purity, tried in the fire, wealth
Negative: Idolatry, greed

GRAY
Positive: Wisdom, maturity
Negative: Unclear, undefined, compromise

GREEN
Positive: New growth, prosperity, environmental, GO!
Negative: Inexperienced (green horn)

HOT PINK
Positive: Visible, fun, playful
Negative: Lust, spirit of Jezebel, control, manipulation

ORANGE
Positive: Fire, purification, energy, fresh vision, new zest for life
Negative: Warning

PINK
Positive: Feminine, child-like, innocence, healing
Negative: Exploitation

PURPLE
Positive: Royalty, Issachar anointing (knowing times and seasons), leadership/building
Negative: Foreign, alien, strange

RED
Positive: Passion, speed
Negative: Warfare, anger, stop

SILVER
Positive: Redemption, refined
Negative: Legalism, law

TEAL
Positive: Color of heaven and kingdom of God's creative glory
Negative: Mixture, cannot stand as pure in hue

WHITE
<u>Positive:</u> Purity, righteousness, innocence, clean, winter
<u>Negative:</u> Without hue, empty, blank
YELLOW
<u>Positive:</u> Gift of God, light, sun, optimism, romance
<u>Negative:</u> Fear, caution, denial

Made in the USA
Lexington, KY
27 October 2019